What people are saying about …

RECLAIMING SANITY

"In *Reclaiming Sanity*, Dr. Shaler addresses some of the most painful questions we face in life with compassion and tenderness. She offers both practical insight from her many years of clinical experience and biblical nourishment for the weary soul. If you or a loved one is suffering, Dr. Shaler has written this book to bring you helpful coping tactics, spiritual encouragement, and most of all, hope."

Katherine and Jay Wolf, coauthors
and cofounders of Hope Heals

"Laurel Shaler speaks with the authority of a professional counselor and the kindness of a caring friend. Her words provide not only hope and inspiration but practical, life-changing application."

Holley Gerth, bestselling author
of *You're Already Amazing*

"You can get beyond it all and live free again. Emotional distress and trauma in life can leave one more than unsettled—it can destroy a sense of safety and stability. In *Reclaiming Sanity*, Dr.

Shaler takes you on a healing journey through and past the pain using careful clinical wisdom that is always anchored in Christ."

Dr. Tim and Julie Clinton, American Association of Christian Counselors President and Extraordinary Women President

"I love how my friend Dr. Laurel Shaler meets you in *Reclaiming Sanity* right where you are. What a powerful message of hope, healing, and redemption. If you've ever been told how you should feel, the healing balm of feeling personally understood in these pages will resonate. With great appreciation for the help it will bring to many people, I recommend this book."

Lisa Whittle, speaker and author of *I Want God* and *Put Your Warrior Boots On*

RECLAIMING SANITY

RECLAIMING SANITY

HOPE and HEALING for TRAUMA, STRESS, and OVERWHELMING LIFE EVENTS

DR. LAUREL SHALER

RECLAIMING SANITY
Published by David C Cook
4050 Lee Vance Drive
Colorado Springs, CO 80918 U.S.A.

David C Cook U.K., Kingsway Communications
Eastbourne, East Sussex BN23 6NT, England

The graphic circle C logo is a registered trademark of David C Cook.

The website addresses recommended throughout this book are offered as a
resource to you. These websites are not intended in any way to be or imply an
endorsement on the part of David C Cook, nor do we vouch for their content.

Unless otherwise noted, all Scripture references are taken from Holy Bible, NEW
INTERNATIONAL VERSION®, NIV®. Copyright © 1973, 2011 by Biblica, Inc.®
Used by permission. All rights reserved worldwide. NEW INTERNATIONAL
VERSION® and NIV® are registered trademarks of Biblica, Inc. Use of either
trademark for the offering of goods or services requires the prior written consent of
Biblica, Inc. Scripture quotations marked NLT are taken from the *Holy Bible*, New
Living Translation, copyright © 1996, 2007 by Tyndale House Foundation. Used
by permission of Tyndale House Publishers, Inc., Carol Stream, Illinois 60188. All
rights reserved. The author has added italics to Scripture quotations for emphasis.

PUBLISHER'S NOTE: This book is not intended to replace a one-on-one
relationship with a qualified health care professional, but as a sharing of knowledge
and information from the research and experience of the author. You are advised
and encouraged to consult with your health care professional in all matters
relating to your health and the health of your family. The publisher and author
disclaim any liability arising directly or indirectly from the use of this book.
AUTHOR'S NOTE: This book contains numerous case examples. In
order to preserve the privacy of the people involved, we have disguised
their appearances, names, and personal stories so that they are not
identifiable. Case examples may also include composite characters.

LCCN 2017931091
ISBN 978-1-4347-1042-0
eISBN 978-1-4347-1051-2

© 2017 Dr. Laurel Shaler
Published in association with literary agent Diana Flegal of
Hartline Literary Agency. www.hartlineliterary.com.
The Team: Alice Crider, Nick Lee, Jack Campbell, Susan Murdock
Cover Design: Amy Konyndyk
Cover Photo: Getty Images

Printed in the United States of America
First Edition 2017

1 2 3 4 5 6 7 8 9 10

032917

This book is dedicated to every woman who is hurting because of a difficult life event. My prayer for you all, loved ones, former clients, and strangers, is that you will know that neither height nor depth, nor anything else in all creation, will ever be able to separate you from the love of God. May these words from Romans 8:39 provide comfort and peace as you seek the root source of all healing: Jesus.

And to my mother, the strongest woman I know.

The Spirit of the Sovereign LORD is on me, because the LORD has anointed me to proclaim good news to the poor. He has sent me to bind up the brokenhearted, to proclaim freedom for the captives and release from darkness for the prisoners, to proclaim the year of the LORD's favor and the day of vengeance of our God, to comfort all who mourn, and provide for those who grieve in Zion—to bestow on them a crown of beauty instead of ashes, the oil of joy instead of mourning, and a garment of praise instead of a spirit of despair. They will be called oaks of righteousness, a planting of the LORD for the display of his splendor.

Isaiah 61:1–3

CONTENTS

Part IV: Reclaiming Sanity

INTRODUCTION

YOUR PATH TOWARD HEALING

You wake in the middle of the night feeling afraid. Maybe you can't even get to sleep … at least not without the lights on.

You startle easily and can't shake the feeling that something bad is going to happen.

You worry. You're sad. You feel guilty. You get so angry you can't think straight.

You're trying hard to deal with it all, but your coping skills aren't the best.

The worst part is, you may have no idea why you feel the way you do.

Everyone recognizes combat and sexual assaults as traumatic events that affect those who experience them, but what about other tough, life-altering events? No one gets through life unscathed. We all face stressful, overwhelming, even traumatic experiences. Can you be traumatized as a result of an ugly divorce? An abortion? A car accident? The simple and short answer to these questions is: *yes*. And don't let anyone tell you (including well-meaning pastors and mental health professionals) how you "should" feel or think after a bad experience. Instead, find those who are willing to come alongside of you in this journey back to peace and joy.

If You Need Help Right Now

If you feel suicidal or think you might hurt yourself or another, call 1-800-273-8255

www.suicidepreventionlifeline.org

You should also seek help *immediately* if you:

- feel you are "coming apart"
- are no longer in control
- are about to do something you may later regret
- have a history of emotional disturbance
- turn to alcohol, drugs, or other addictive substances
- feel isolated with no one to turn to

If you are seeking a licensed mental health professional who offers Christian counseling, you can locate one at www.aacc.net/resources/find-a-counselor/.

Thankfully, most people who go through a traumatic experience *don't* develop post-traumatic stress disorder. This is good news! *Of the less than 10 percent who do develop PTSD, effective, evidence-based treatment is available.* **However, many people unknowingly suffer as a result of a traumatic experience.** Problems develop that disrupt our daily lives, our jobs, our relationships, and even our health.

What about those more hidden, private, but just as common events? Was your faith shaken when your child was diagnosed with mental illness? Maybe you experience lingering upsetting thoughts that disrupt your ability to concentrate or to leave the house, that bring on long crying spells from the loss of a loved one or from a miscarriage.

These events can leave you feeling wrecked, out of control, or overwhelmed—as if you've come unmoored. They can make you wonder if you're maybe even certifiably crazy. If you have asked, "What is going on with me?" or "Why can't I get over this?" or you know of someone else who has, this book is for you. Regardless of what you are feeling, **there is hope and healing for what you're going through.** While we explore the causes and symptoms associated with experiencing a traumatic event (or a series of them), and the impact it can have on your life, you will also learn how to access Jesus Christ as your source of strength and healing. I have journeyed alongside women who've undergone great tragedy and stress, who are now living in freedom and hope. The journey is not easy, but the truth is: If God is for you, who can be against you (Romans 8:31)? No one; not even yourself.

HOW TO USE THIS BOOK

While envisioning this book, I envisioned you. I am praying for you. While my desire is to meet you personally in my living room and drink tea and eat chocolate imported from London, I'm glad we are together here, listening to the words of Jesus about what He has to say to you. God is timeless, and His truth is too. I would even go so far as to say that God has orchestrated this book for you today. I believe *Reclaiming Sanity* has been directed by the hand of our Lord "for such a time as this" so that you might know the depths and heights of His love and great promise for you.

I love a good story, and you'll find many of them here. What makes a story good? A life with hills and valleys and battles and victories, but also one that has been transformed, healed, and renewed. While studying the book of Luke in Sunday school, I was reminded of how profoundly Jesus liberated women. We simply do not find examples of Jesus and women facing off with conflict in the Gospels. Jesus loved women, healed them, served them, saved them—and He does today too! He came from God through a woman, and women were the first to see Him resurrected and the first He spoke to. Jesus loves women!

A good story is one that is infused with hope. The names of women within these pages have been changed as well as some details to protect their identities, but the core of each story carries its original remarkable truth. I have given extra care to refrain from triggers in the vignettes and narratives that might otherwise cause pain.

While the concepts here may seem familiar at first glance (intentionally so), I hope you will pause and give each one a moment more of your attention and see how the stories, questions, and exercises might influence your life. This is a book to be used, not merely to be read.

Reclaiming Sanity is a self-guided journey. Take your time to ensure you thoroughly grasp the concept of each section and chapter before moving on to the next. You may even want to go through some chapters, or sections of chapters, more than once. Each chapter offers a combination of scriptures, questions, and/or practice activities to help you explore the concepts we are talking about. I encourage you to look up each scripture and answer the questions provided, as these will help guide you in choosing a path of healing and hope with the strength that can come only from God.

UPCOMING SECTIONS AND CHAPTERS

The fact that you are here is a good indication that you or a loved one is suffering, but you are choosing to do whatever you can to survive, heal, grow, live, and maybe even love again. Part I: Reclaiming Clarity opens with chapter 1 asking the question I often hear, "Am I going crazy?" Numerous sources indicate that one-half to two-thirds of adults have experienced a traumatic experience at some point in their lives. In addition to combat and sexual trauma, there are many other sources of trauma that people do not consider to have a lasting impact. Divorce, death of a loved one, loss of a job, and other life events can remain with us longer than we expect. No wonder you're feeling crazy! I know the feeling, and I share a little bit about that in my personal story found in chapter 2. Regardless of what you've been through or what you are in the middle of right now, *you're not alone*. In chapter 3, we'll talk about the hidden epidemic of trauma and the power of choosing, and about journeying alongside Jesus, who bears our greatest burdens with us.

Next, we'll take a look at what trauma is and what trauma isn't. How do we distinguish between good stress, bad stress, and being overwhelmed? What about post-traumatic stress disorder (PTSD)? How do we know if that's what we are dealing with? Chapters 4 and 5 will help define terms and treatments of PTSD and its precursor, acute stress disorder (ASD). If you've come to believe that there is little hope of long-term change and healing, then chapter 6, "More than a Band-Aid," is for you.

Are you ready to see remarkable and lasting change? Part II: Reclaiming Me (chapters 7 through 12) is a powerful section. Troubling emotions are often masked by frustration and anger, which means it's time to wrestle this monster down to the ground and get a good look at what you're dealing with. Where are you now and where do you want to be? Have you gotten lost or do you feel defined by what happened? Who or what seems to be the obstacle you are fighting? Dealing with emotions is a big part of reclaiming our truest identity in Jesus and the truth about who we are. Are you ready to break the chains of reaction so that you are no longer perpetuating trauma and stress or overwhelming situations? In chapter 12 you will find your truest identity. You may want to read it first and then read it again after you've read the earlier chapters.

Part III: Reclaiming Peace is about beginning again, turning your heart outward, being a participant in hope and peace, finding the freedom in forgiveness, rebuilding relationships, and solving problems mindfully.

Part IV: Reclaiming Sanity provides ideas and resources so you can throw out a lifeline to help trauma survivors, including yourself. There is important information in this section about secondary trauma, which is stress or symptoms associated with helping or living with someone who has experienced trauma directly. The capstone, chapter 18, "Reimagine," is a mini retreat that is sure to bring you or your small group to a place of relaxation and rest as you learn to take care of yourself in the most luxurious ways possible. And you don't even have to pay those expensive spa prices!

Since the beginning of time, humanity has been given the gift of choice. In fact, choice plays a pivotal role in God's big story with us. You were fashioned to participate with Jesus, who was present at the creation of the world and is in the ongoing creative process of your life. It should come as no surprise, then, that choice is at the very heart of the path to restoration and peace. You were designed with the power and guidance of God's Word and the prompting of the Holy Spirit to choose your thoughts and behavior. It is a difficult journey, but one filled with hope. You can reclaim who you were designed to be. You *can* reclaim sanity.

CHAPTER 1

AM I GOING CRAZY?

"The LORD is close to the brokenhearted
and saves those who are crushed in spirit."

Psalm 34:18

In addition to combat and sexual trauma, many other sources of
suffering affect us that go unaddressed—maybe even unrecognized—
because our culture does not readily acknowledge the weight or
lasting impact of losses, such as divorce, death of a loved one, loss of
a job, a miscarriage, and other life events, that can remain with us
longer than what others think they should. Experiencing any of these,
or other traumatic events, can lead to thoughts and feelings that may
make us feel crazy. In this chapter, we discuss stress, overwhelming
events, and trauma, and identify the difference between them. We'll
also discuss the various symptoms these three cause. And you'll receive
this good news: you're not going crazy.

"What is going on with me?"

"Why am I restless and afraid?"

"How can I get over this?"

Sometimes we can't determine for ourselves the difference between what is typical and what is out of control; what is good stress and what is bad stress; what is a wayward belief and what is a warning sign. Is this a warning sign or an irrational fear; "healthy" grief or harmful? Although there is no rule about what is "normal," sometimes it is helpful to have some guidelines and definition of terms to bring about clarity.

1	3	5	7	8	9	10

"Ever After" fantasy – Life Challenge – stressful situations (good/bad) – distress – overwhelmed – trauma – debilitating trauma

If you have ever wondered how an event or relationship that happened so long ago can still be bothering you, it's possible you've experienced a trauma that is affecting you more than you realize. For a moment, think back over your life. Have you gone through something really tough? Sure, we've all gone through challenging situations, but I mean an accident, incident, or crisis that was *really* painful. Could it have been difficult enough to result in lingering thoughts, feelings, or behaviors that are troubling and maybe even dangerous? These questions can be a bit subjective. In other words, what I consider a traumatic event may not be what you would consider one, and vice versa. Before we talk further about levels of distress, let me tell you what trauma is *not*.

WHAT TRAUMA IS *NOT*

While traveling through a small town, I decided to stop for some dinner. I rushed in to use the ladies' room before heading to the buffet. As I was piling food onto my plate, a young male waiter came up to me and whispered, "Ma'am, you've got some toilet paper hanging out of the back of your pants." Go ahead, I hear you laughing. But wait. It gets worse (or better, depending on your perspective). I grabbed the tissue and made a beeline to a booth, hoping to fade into obscurity (which wasn't hard to do since the place was all but vacant).

Pushing my embarrassment away, I dug into my chicken and mashed potatoes with fervor, wanting to get back on the road. Just then a pair of boots ambled by, stopped, and backed up next to where I was sitting. With fork midway to my mouth, I glanced up to see a middle-aged truck driver standing there shaking his head. "Ma'am," he said. (What's up with all the "ma'ams"?) I sat my fork down, then dabbed my mouth with a napkin before giving him a big doe-eyed questioning glance, to which he stated, "There's still some down there."

My face turned hot as embarrassment washed over me again. You may be half-groaning and half-laughing, recalling your own mortifying moments. Still, as devastating as that pit stop was, the situation was not traumatic. Of course, humiliation (and repeated humiliation) may very well lead to suffering. But this was not one of those cases.

Although trauma can be subjective (excluding a formal PTSD diagnosis, wherein each criterion in the *Diagnostic*

Statistical Manual must be met), I am convinced that we must be cautious about mislabeling. If we identify any and every thing that goes wrong in our lives as traumatic, we not only allow ourselves to be victimized by frustrations and hardships, but we reduce the meaning of trauma. On the other hand, if we fail to recognize that bad things happen that affect or injure us, sometimes for many years, we are minimizing the impact of the trauma.

What else is trauma *not*? Trauma is not rare.

WHAT TRAUMA *IS*

Trauma *is* one of the world's leading epidemics. Yet it most often remains hidden. According to the National Center for PTSD, five out of ten women, and six out of ten men experience a traumatic event in their lives.[1] Think about that for a minute: 50 percent of women and 60 percent of men experience what Merriam-Webster's defines as "a very difficult or unpleasant experience that causes someone to have mental or emotional problems, usually for a long time."[2]

When we think of trauma, we almost always think about acute stress disorder (ASD) and post-traumatic stress disorder (PTSD). To be sure, ASD, which can lead to PTSD, and PTSD are both real, and we will explore them in chapter 4, but first, let's focus on the scenarios we too often ignore that affect all of us deeply—events that cause problematic thoughts, feelings, and behaviors that do not fit neatly into the PTSD box.

What can be identified as trauma, other than events that we can all agree are traumatic—such as combat and sexual assault? I mentioned some examples of trauma in the introduction, and others include: physical abuse, a house fire, a car accident, surviving a tornado or hurricane, the loss of a child, and facing a life-or-death surgery. Less obvious examples, such as emotional abuse, severe or chronic illness or pain (life threatening or not), witnessing something severe happening to another person, living under the threat of war, and experiencing the unexpected or untimely death of a loved one, often go unnoticed.

For most people, recovery from traumatic events happens naturally and on a timely basis. For others, not so much. Have you experienced an incident listed here—or one not listed—and noticed that you are struggling with your thoughts, feelings, or behaviors? Have you wondered why you are moping around? Are you concerned about the cause of your sleep difficulties? Tired of being afraid that something bad is going to happen? Sick of being frustrated or irritable? If you find yourself isolating or avoiding others or doing things you wouldn't ordinarily do (an obvious example would be using drugs or alcohol to cope), **you may be dealing with the hidden epidemic of trauma.**

After reading about trauma, you still may not be sure whether any of this applies to you. Maybe you feel too numb and disconnected to care. If so, the following quiz can help identify what is at the root of your troubling emotions and actions. There are two short parts to this quiz, with seven questions for you to answer in the first part, and six in the second part, followed by an explanation of results.

THE TRAUMA QUIZ

Part I

Y   N   Have you survived a natural disaster (flood, hurricane, tornado, etc.)?

Y   N   Have you been in a car accident or house fire?

Y   N   Have you witnessed something really bad happen to someone else?

Y   N   Has someone in your life died suddenly, unnaturally, or untimely?

Y   N   Has someone assaulted or abused you emotionally, physically, or sexually?

Y   N   Have you been bullied or betrayed?

Y   N   Has anything bad happened in your life that still bothers you?

Part II

Y   N   Do you have emotions you can't explain?

Y   N   Do you get angry or frustrated for unknown reasons?

Y   N   Do you feel like you're going crazy?

Y   N   Are you having upsetting thoughts related to a negative experience?

Y   N   Are you involved in behaviors that started after a negative event that are out of the ordinary for you?

Y   N   Are you sick and tired of feeling emotionally down all the time?

Note: This quiz is not intended to take the place of testing conducted by a mental health professional, nor is it intended to be used as a diagnostic instrument.

Results

If you answered yes to at least one question in part I and yes to at least one question in part II of the Trauma Quiz, you may be living in the aftermath of a traumatic life event. More importantly, if you answered yes to any of these questions, you have survived! Survival is not a place to remain, however. Surviving is a necessary step in healing, but it is not fully living. Remember that there is hope for living fully, and the next steps to healing are offered within these pages.

WHAT IS STRESS?

You've probably heard the word *stress* used to describe many different scenarios. In fact, you've probably been "stressed out" more times than you can count. Merriam-Webster's defines stress simply as "a state of mental tension and worry caused by problems in your life."[3] But did you know there are two major types of stress? There's good stress, *eustress*, and there's bad stress, *distress*.

Eustress (pronounced "u-stress") is what you experience when a positive disruption happens in your life that, even though it is "good," is difficult to cope with emotionally. Some life situations that may lead to eustress include having a baby, graduating from high school, starting college, buying your first home, receiving a job promotion, getting married—and the list goes on! Researchers from Brock University say eustress can help people be "motivated, challenged, and productive."[4]

Distress, on the other hand, includes those all-too-frequent negative, upsetting feelings that accompany the bad stuff going on. Whereas eustress can foster needed energy and hope, distress takes hold when people don't see any resolution or end in sight. As a result, the individual may undergo problematic physical and behavioral symptoms such as high blood pressure, tension, changes in appetite, and more. It is possible to feel distress over a positive life situation too, if one gets to the point of having difficulty handling all of the resulting changes, responsibilities, etc., but distress is more often experienced as a result of negative occurrences. The sudden or ongoing stressful encounters you've had may still be affecting you today. Stress can make you feel overwhelmed. Read on to learn more about that.

WHAT IS AN OVERWHELMING LIFE EVENT?

"I'm so overwhelmed!" I exclaimed to my husband. We were buying a house, I was struggling through a disagreement with a dear friend, and I had tons of work to do. Can you relate? You have so much going on in life that you almost don't know where to begin. You wonder how or if you'll get things under control. You may feel anxious or close to panic—as if hiding under your work desk would make the whole world disappear, at least for a little while.

You wake up with a sinking feeling and can't figure out why, until suddenly you're reminded of a past or present event, or series of events, that engulfs you with powerful emotion. When overwhelmed, you feel plagued with chaotic thoughts, memories, and feelings. Your anxiety may rise to the point that you want to escape entirely because you believe it's all too much. At a minimum, you don't want to face a mountain of demands. Perhaps you don't know *how* to face them.

If you experienced a combination of life events that left you feeling trounced, the initial anxiety or excessive worry you felt during the original experience may remain. Feeling overwhelmed is similar to having chronic flashbacks—that experience of reliving the negative event—wherein you don't know how to channel or cope with the onslaught of emotion.

Say you've had a rough day. You got the kids to school late because of a fender bender, your boss gives you "one more chance" to improve your work, and you receive a notice saying that your bank account is overdrawn. When you realize you burned the gourmet pizza (okay, frozen pizza), you start to cry. You've had a life pileup. Hubby starts questioning why you would cry over burned pizza, and you realize it's not about the pizza at all. It's about everything else that took place that day. The stress is cumulative and distressing. Stress can make you feel overwhelmed, as can other emotions, such as anger, anxiety, and depression. We will explore these in more detail later in the book.

GOOD NEWS! YOU'RE *NOT* CRAZY

By understanding the difference between trauma, stress, and over-whelming life events, you can begin recognizing and accepting that something legitimately bad has taken place and that your problematic thoughts, feelings, or behaviors are the *real and expected* results. **This is not about excuse making or justifying wrongdoings; it is merely the first step in choosing to be healed from your past and facing the future in a better place physically, emotionally, and spiritually.** It's real. You have suffered, but you are also being restored. You are getting stronger—not by yourself, but with Christ, who is your strength, and with a community of people who love and care for you. The good news is: you are *not* crazy, even when you may feel like it. The better news is:

Answers are on the way.

Healing has begun.

You are alive.

You are loved.

You are not crazy.

You can reclaim sanity.

CHAPTER 2

THE FOURTEEN-POUND ...

"The LORD is with me; I will not be afraid."
Psalm 118:6

"You need to have this surgery or you will die." Imagine the shock at hearing these words at the tender age of eighteen. Die? I was just getting started with living. I shot a desperate glance over at my mother. Death was nowhere on my horizon. Dr. Mac fiddled with the buttons on his white jacket and peered over his glasses. His eyes lasered a path between my mother's face and mine. What I saw in her eyes made me burst into tears. I reached for my mama's hand.

This was not how the story was supposed to go …

The day before I met Dr. Mac, I'd been to a different doctor for a routine physical required to transfer colleges. I had just completed my first year at a small Christian college, where I'd planned to become a youth minister—in Costa Rica—only, I had never visited that country, and now clearly my heart had outgrown my previous high school dream. When I realized neither Costa Rica nor youth pastoring was my life path, I decided to transfer to a larger college on the coast with many more majors and options. Did I mention the beach? That fateful July, one year after my high school graduation and one month prior to my future, I was almost out of the doctor's door when I decided to mention an odd change in my body.

"Oh, I forgot to mention, for some reason, *my stomach has become really hard*," I said.

The primary care physician asked me to hop back up onto the exam table so he could do a quick check of my tummy. I pulled my tank top up a little. His cool fingers barely touched my abdomen before he said flatly, "There's something wrong here. You need an ultrasound. Now."

I was sent directly to the radiologist's office for an abdominal ultrasound. Before the radiology technician even touched me, she said, "I already know what's wrong with you. You've got a big ol' cyst in there."

That southern gal was right. The cyst growing on my right ovary was so large that the technician could not adequately measure it. In fact, she asked the radiologist to come and take a look because she was so shocked at the size. Turns out I was packing a cystic tumor—larger than most sets of twins—fourteen pounds. It's okay to gasp. After all these years, I still do.

On the way to the hospital on surgery day, I wore a T-shirt that said "Fear Not" and kept repeating Romans 8:31 over and over and over again: "If God is for me, who can be against me?"

I was absolutely *terrified*.

I had never experienced anything like this before and simply had no idea what the outcome was going to be. Still, the apostle Paul's words brought me great comfort. I still have my "Fear Not" T-shirt, now a soft, faded black, gray, and red on a white background as a reminder of God's favor that day.

Waking up from surgery, I blinked back the lights shining behind my daddy's six-foot frame. "I made it," I whispered.

"Of course you did," he said as he bent his head close to mine. I know that neither of us had been so sure prior to the surgery.

While the physical recovery after such a complicated procedure was tough, even with a wonderful support system of parents, friends, and church members, the emotional recovery was much tougher. In addition to the typical discomforts of healing from a major surgery, I had raging hot flashes for more than two years after my surgery (during which time I developed a lot of empathy for women going through menopause). I lived part of that time in an old apartment building that had one of those ancient heating-air units. During those hot flashes, I felt as if I were on fire from the inside out. Without warning, I'd be engulfed, broiling, so I'd draped myself *across the top* of the air conditioner. And I'd still be burning up! Yet even though these and other physical symptoms were rough, the emotional recovery was much worse—and hidden, because I kept silent.

I couldn't describe or name it at the time, but I now know that I was dealing with anxiety and excessive worry. During those first few months after surgery, there were times when I couldn't eat because I felt so uneasy and upset. The anxious nausea would come in waves. I would be starving at lunchtime, but as soon as I unwrapped my chicken soft taco, my appetite vanished. I would become fearful, sometimes over the least little physical concern and sometimes for unknown reasons. At times I even struggled to breathe, which I blamed on my adolescent asthma.

I now know that much of my emotional turmoil was a result of trauma. But all this took place before I could put a word to that terrible feeling. Even though I wasn't continually having conscious thoughts, such as *Something else is wrong with me* or *I might have died*, my brain knew and reported this information to my body. Hence the loss of appetite, the fear sensation, the breathing difficulty, and more. Still, when I think what might have happened had I not stopped at the exam room door—about how close the cyst was to rupturing and how it would have over-whelmed my body, much like a burst appendix—to turn around and ask the doctor about my expanding, rock-hard stomach after he had already wrapped up his physical exam (yeah, how did he miss that?), well, that makes the breathing even tougher.

LITTLE "T" VERSUS BIG "T"

As a counselor and educator, having now worked with survivors of trauma for many years and seeing the way severe distress affects innumerable unknowing survivors, I have discovered that my desire is to help women understand and recognize trauma. One way to look at the difference between the stressors of life and the big issues of life is to look at little "t" trauma versus big "T" trauma.

While I wouldn't call my incredibly embarrassing moment of being caught *twice* with toilet paper sticking out of my pants Traumatic, it was stressful and slightly traumatic—little "t." Though I certainly don't want a repeat performance, and it takes some time to recover from little "t" humiliating experiences such as mine, these scenarios are not nearly as tough or challenging to recover from as the big "T" traumas.

While shedding light on this topic, I see the need to help those who have issues related to recognized Trauma *and* unrecognized Trauma, and to address the PTSD and non-PTSD problems that can arise as a result. The reality is: being female increases the risk of developing PTSD, a well-established fact in the trauma field. Additionally, experts Raabe and Spengler claim, "A history of child abuse and maltreatment increases the likelihood of being subsequently exposed to traumatic events or of developing PTSD as an adult."[1]

However, it doesn't have to go that way. Our past doesn't have to—doesn't *get* to—dictate our future. And being a woman doesn't mean we are bound to experience never-ending struggle as a result of trauma.

CHAPTER 3

YOU'RE NOT ALONE

"I cry aloud to the LORD; I lift up my voice to the LORD for mercy.
I pour out before him my complaint; before him I tell my trouble."

Psalm 142:1–2

It is common to feel alone in the midst of dark times in our lives. Yet,
as King David did in the psalm above, we can cry out to God. In this
chapter, we explore answers to questions you may have about suffering,
and how God fits into this part of life. You may feel abandoned, but
I want to remind you of God's great promise that you're never alone.

KATE AND FRAN'S STORY

One night, Kate and a coworker, Fran, both wound up in the inten-
sive care unit (ICU) with their husbands. Both of their spouses
were in critical condition, both for heart-related concerns. Kate
and Fran sat in the waiting room together through the long hours

of the night, drinking black vending-machine coffee and whispering their fears to each other. In an unexpected turn of events, they went from being office acquaintances sharing a laugh and hors d'oeuvres at the annual Christmas party to sharing intimate details of family and life long into the night—until the fateful moment when Fran learned that her husband had passed away.

Kate's husband, Chris, survived, followed by months of hospitalization, numerous surgeries, and a lengthy rehabilitation stay before going home. Each day was grueling and exhausting, one twenty-four-hour period blurring into the next; still, Kate never stopped thanking God that her husband of almost two decades was still alive.

Eventually the day came when Kate saw Fran, walking toward her at work. She dipped her head, feeling awkward and uncomfortable. Fran's eyes filled with tears when she asked about Chris. Kate appreciated Fran's concern but couldn't help thinking about the close call she had faced—and the reality of loss her colleague had suffered. As a result, whenever Kate saw Fran at work, Kate felt afraid, worried, even panicked.

Sometimes, Kate wakes up in the middle of the night sweating and terrified of what could have been—and what might still be. Chris survived, but one day he still has to die. At times, these fretful thoughts consume her. She is thankful for her husband's ongoing progress but hasn't fully processed the trauma she faced that night in the ICU or the months of ups and downs since that time. Kate describes the two weeks that Chris was comatose as "dark, dark days" waiting for her husband to wake up. She read Habakkuk 3:17–18 to him each day, relying on the promise that even though all appeared to be lost, "My God was still worthy of praise and I had reasons to rejoice." Kate sang songs, read Scripture, and surrounded herself with people who brought her comfort.

Because of her faith and amazing community of support, Kate may or may not meet diagnostic criteria for PTSD, but she certainly has felt the impact of trauma. Although she is grateful her husband survived, she feels guilty for feeling anxious, not to mention her loneliness in her struggle. Sometimes when we are surrounded by people, even loving and supportive people, we may still feel utterly alone. And even though we *know* the truth about God's sovereignty and love, we might not *feel* God's presence.

DEEP LONELINESS

In particular, during times of tragedy, we may ask the bold question that Judy Blume's well-known 1970s character, Margaret, asked: "Are you there, God?" Since the fall of humanity in the garden of Eden, the world has been broken by sin and hardship. Although suffering is common and universal, we often feel alone. No other human can possibly understand, and God … where is God in the midst of this pain? We may even feel like we pray and nothing changes, including feeling like we're all alone. Let's take a look at this feeling of loneliness and how God and others can be involved in our healing.

When I teach future counselors basic counseling skills, I strongly advise against telling clients these two loaded words: "I understand." I explain that even if the counselor has been through a similar experience as what the client has, the counselor is not in the exact same place as the one seeking help. Though many similarities may be found, just as many differences in experiences remain. While a counselor can express hearing and understanding what the client is communicating, and while one should certainly be empathetic, he or she cannot truly understand the client's unique experiences.

On one hand, we are affirmed in our unique suffering, but on the other, *the sense that no one else truly understands what we're going through in that moment contributes to the loneliness.* As a result, when women experience rough or traumatic times in life, they may want to hide behind a mask so that others don't know what they're really going through. Seemingly, the mask doesn't matter because no one will understand anyway.

Others won't fully understand, but we all need support. While there are varying degrees of injury and harm that we endure, there is connection and community in the fact that others have been through rough times too. We find kinship in suffering. It is a well-known fact that being with others who have had similar journeys is a primary benefit offered by support groups. It is quite another to actually be daring and vulnerable enough to join one (more on this in chapter 4). So, while others may not completely understand, they can be a great resource for you. Perhaps they have been through a similar experience and can give you helpful tips or resources. Maybe they have experienced a completely different traumatic event, but they know what it's like to feel alone or be alone. Maybe they will just be there, a friend on the journey. Isolating yourself from everyone will only further your loneliness. You need support; don't shy away from it.

"WHY, O LORD?"

But what about God? How can we trust a person or relationship without knowing the character and makeup of whomever we are being asked to trust? I sure can't! Trust issues are common among those who have experienced trauma or overwhelming life events. Who is God and how (and why) should we find comfort in this God we can't physically see? We trust God for our eternal salvation, but what about right now? This is the beauty of the Bible; it is the story of God's everlasting love and patience for humanity, and His coming for us. It tells the story of God's presence with us in our greatest time of suffering. Yes, He's most certainly been through suffering too. You can be sure that God cares about your suffering because He's been there.

God, the Father, and Jesus, the Son, both experienced tremendous suffering at the cross. God sent His only Son to die a horrific death, and Jesus endured the physical pain of the cross and the emotional pain of our sin. The reality is that God is good. After creating heaven, earth, day, night, water, land, trees, stars, animals, and humans—with freedom of choice and dominion over everything—sin entered the world. God intended for His creation to live forever, and He provided for their every need. Yet, the first two humans were not content to be given everything except for one tree they were commanded not to touch.

Eve, and then Adam, was tempted by Satan, the great deceiver, and gave in to the temptation. As a result, sin entered the world. Satan has not let up since. It's tempting to ask why, if God is loving, He would allow bad things to happen to people. The answer is complex, but the bottom line is we live in a fallen world filled with sin because of humankind's broken nature. Sometimes it's our own sin that leads to painful consequences (we steal money from our employer and go to prison), and sometimes it's the sin of others (a drunk driver hits and kills a loved one). And sometimes we have no explanation except for the fact that the world has not been perfect since the original sin was committed. We have a choice as to whether we will be intimidated by the world.

We may be able to understand why we have to deal with the results of our own wrongdoings (and thankful for God's forgiveness), but it's harder to accept that we are left to deal with the results of the wrongdoings of others. Even more incomprehensible is when appalling things happen when no one has sinned (such as a child being diagnosed with cancer). I certainly don't have all the answers, but I know that this world is temporary. Jesus even promises us we'll have trouble (John 16:33), but He goes on to tell us to take heart because He has overcome the world. He doesn't relish our suffering; instead, He's made a way for us to have peace in this world, to accompany us in our suffering and to give us eternal life after we leave this world. I love the words of Hebrews 12:28, which states, "Therefore, since we are receiving a kingdom that cannot be shaken, let us be thankful, and so worship God acceptably with reverence and awe."

The truth is that bad things happen to *all* people, and all people are sinners in need of salvation. When bad things happen (whether by our own behaviors or as a result of others), *we have a choice*. We can run to God knowing He is the only One who can truly understand our pain, or we can turn away from Him and depend on our own limited ideas to deliver us. We have options, a choice to make. Do you want to live dictated by your past, or do you want to lean into the work of the Master Creator and toward the future? To move toward Jesus and His redemptive work is always to lean into the future.

Perhaps you've heard Jeremiah 29:11 so many times that the words have become trite, but I suggest reading them again. Slowly, carefully, absorbing every word: "'For I know the plans I have for you,' declares the LORD, 'plans to prosper you and not to harm you, plans to give you hope and a future.'" God's plans give us a future. What kind of future do you want?

For Kate, she reached out for professional help because she wanted that good future. She knew she needed help in order to control her worry and her sleepless nights. She wanted to focus on her gratitude toward God for saving her husband, and she wanted to spend more time enjoying being with him than spending time feeling anxious over what happened, what could have happened, or what may happen in the future. While Kate couldn't understand why her husband was spared and Fran's husband wasn't, her desire was to trust God, the Sovereign One who created them all, so she turned to the Word of God daily.

In moments when Kate and Chris experienced great uncertainty, they were also able to find joy. And while Kate still has occasional waves of ugly emotions crash over her, she is better prepared to ride those waves or allow them to roll on over. She accepts that this may be a part of life for a while … or forever, but she chooses to focus on the hope and the future that God has promised and provided. In place of sadness and regret over what was lost, they celebrate the milestones along the journey of recovery. And they worship God for what He has done.

BUILDING A MONUMENT TO GOD'S FAITHFUL LOVE

When people have experienced something terrible, and they see, hear, taste, or smell a reminder of their bad experience, that sensory event can trigger negative symptoms, thoughts, feelings, and behaviors. Though these experiences can be traumatic in and of themselves, one is not left powerless and without options. We can choose to take an otherwise terrible reminder of the past and turn it into a monument—a physical place with significance—of God's faithful presence.

Monuments are all around us, and many exist that support the Bible's historical accuracy. For example, in the 1990s, a broken stone tablet was found at Tel Dan in Israel with words that translated to the "House of David." This was the first physical evidence that King David existed. While Christians already believed in this important Old Testament character, this was a reminder of how what God says is indeed true. We can also use physical items and places to remind us of God's faithfulness. Instead of allowing these reminders to conjure up pain, have you considered molding them into new monuments that remind you of how far God has brought you? Perhaps these ideas will get you started:

- Instead of allowing a route by the hospital to bring you into the pit of sadness or worry over what happened or could have happened there, think about how far the Lord has taken you since that time.
- Instead of diving headfirst into grief and guilt as you drive past the clinic where you had an abortion, reflect on the forgiveness offered to you through Christ, and how you can get involved in helping other women prevent or recover from similar pain.
- Instead of hiding under the bed or in the closet at the sound of those fireworks that remind you of gunfire and bombs, go outside and watch them going off (they won't surprise you as much if you know when they are going to explode), knowing that you helped protect the freedoms that those celebratory fireworks represent.

I know the approach to building monuments is much easier said than done, but you can make this one of your goals; one intentional step toward healing and reclaiming sanity. You can learn to remind yourself that something that happened in the past isn't happening right now. And something that might happen in the future isn't happening right now either. (However, if you are in the midst of trauma that these suggestions don't relieve, please seek out safety and help as soon as possible!)

I love the book *When God Weeps* by Joni Eareckson Tada and Steven Estes. The book is amazing—written from Joni's intimate experience of suffering, which gives her special understanding of God's intentions for us in our pain. From our perspective, suffering doesn't make sense, and the authors ask the hard questions beyond the scope of this work, such as "If God is loving, why is there suffering?" I highly recommend the book, and I mention it here because, by the title alone, we are reminded that God promises to be with us, to befriend us; God weeps with us.

We worship and love a Savior who suffers with us. We saw the face of God when Jesus wept for Lazarus even though Jesus knew He was going to bring Lazarus back to life. He was fully present in that moment with Mary and Martha in their great and terrible sadness. Sister, you may feel alone, but Immanuel, Jesus who lived on earth from birth to adulthood, came to show us the face of God, and then He sent His Presence to be with us: a counselor, guide, friend—closer than our very breath. God is with us.[1] As you meditate on the Word of God by letting the written truth descend from your mind into the very core of your being, listen to these words that Jesus promised until they become a part of who you are:

You are not alone.

God is with you.

He has promised you hope and a future.

He will not fail to fulfill His promises.

CHAPTER 4

UNDERSTANDING POST-TRAUMATIC STRESS DISORDER (PTSD)

"Be merciful to me, LORD, for I am in distress;
my eyes grow weak with sorrow, my soul and body with grief.
My life is consumed by anguish and my years by groaning;
my strength fails because of my affliction, and my bones grow weak."

Psalm 31:9–10

This chapter reviews the symptoms of PTSD and the various treatment options that research has proven to be effective for PTSD. The good news is that less than 10 percent of people who have experienced traumatic events develop PTSD. Even better, there are several evidence-based forms of therapy that can help people who have this disorder. These treatments are explored with a following discussion about how Christians can look at this diagnosis, thus weakening its stigma.

Most people equate *trauma* with *post-traumatic stress disorder* (PTSD), and often one term is substituted or used as the other. The assumption is erroneously made that people who experience a traumatic event automatically develop PTSD; and a similar prevailing belief is that PTSD is the *only* problem that results from trauma. While none of this is true, PTSD is very real.

TIA'S STORY

When Tia came to see me, she was upset that she couldn't "shake something that had happened" to her, and she felt guilty that it was hijacking her life with her children. She worried that she wasn't available for her teens, and she felt bad specifically that some nights all they had for dinner was cereal. As her therapist, I thought Tia was doing a pretty good job, in particular because she was still emotionally recovering from having been shot by her husband after years of domestic violence. Thankfully, she got out of the situation before she was killed, but she still struggled significantly as a result of the trauma she endured.

No longer able to work, Tia was determined to survive and make a life for her children, but after years of fear, worry, and nightmares, she knew she needed help. Tia had PTSD. When she came to see me, she met all the diagnostic criteria and had developed an acute stress reaction prior to meeting the one-month criteria for the PTSD diagnosis. While trauma is not rare (at a rate of 50 percent of women and 60 percent of men), developing PTSD is much less common at only around 8 percent. Why do some people recover naturally from trauma while others, like Tia, develop PTSD? Before diving into that, let's take a look at what criteria must be met in order to be diagnosed with PTSD.

DIAGNOSTIC CRITERIA AND SYMPTOMS OF PTSD

According to the American Psychiatric Association's *Diagnostic Statistical Manual* (2013), *the triggering event for a diagnosis of PTSD must be exposure to actual or threatened death, serious injury or sexual violation.*[1] The exposure must result from one or more of the following scenarios, in which the individual:

- directly experiences the traumatic event
- witnesses the traumatic event in person
- learns that the traumatic event occurred to a close family member or close friend (with the actual or threatened death being either violent or accidental); or
- experiences firsthand repeated or extreme exposure to aversive details of the traumatic event (not through media, pictures, television, or movies, unless work related).

Without a doubt, Tia met these criteria. She directly experienced a traumatic event when she was intentionally shot by her husband during a domestic dispute. She knew he had a temper, and he'd been aggressive in the past. Still, she had no idea that he was capable of pointing a gun at her and pulling the trigger. Tia didn't know her husband was armed that fateful day when an argument began to escalate. So, after her husband shot her and immediately turned and ran out of the house, she couldn't comprehend at first that she'd been shot. Thankfully, Tia was conscious enough to call 911 before blacking out. She awoke in the hospital with bandages covering her swollen and bruised leg. Since that day, she can't get these images out of her mind, and her daily, painful limp doesn't help.

Following identification of the trigger, several other criteria must be met in order for someone to be diagnosed with this disorder. Let's take a closer look at these. Criteria following the trigger that determines PTSD include: *intrusion symptoms, avoidance, negative thoughts or moods, and alteration of arousal.* Many of these clinical criteria are familiar terms that we use or hear commonly in everyday contexts, without a full understanding of why or how practitioners use them professionally while diagnosing PTSD.

For example, to be diagnosed with PTSD, the person who lives through a traumatic event must experience one or more *intrusion symptoms* such as recurrent memories, distressing dreams, or flashbacks. For Tia, ongoing nightmares, replaying the scenario over and over again leading up to the moment she was shot, haunted her while she slept. Sometimes while she was awake, she would all of a sudden lose sight of her present reality and be thrust back into the traumatic event, as if she was reliving the horror in precise detail all over again. These moments we all recognize as *flashbacks* would leave Tia in a state of panic as she fought to calm herself, reorient, and reconnect with her present space. Tia was experiencing multiple intrusion symptoms.

Another criterion that must be met for PTSD is related to *avoidance*. This can be avoidance of thoughts or feelings or of reminders. Tia was a pro at dodging treatment. While she knew counseling would be helpful, she struggled with intentionally speaking or thinking about her traumatic experience. She did all kinds of maneuvers to forestall any interaction having to do with her painful past. From my time with Tia, I can't say strongly enough here: as understandable as avoidance is, when used as a primary coping skill, it is *not* healthy.

While we sometimes need a momentary escape (like a good movie or book) to get through a rough day, avoidance is a short-term survival mechanism, not an effective means for healing long term. For example, it would make sense for Tia to set aside any thoughts about her traumatic experience while she was playing a game with her daughter or out shoe shopping with her son. However, here's the thing about avoidance: if all we had to do was avoid our negative past experiences in order for them to go away, they would be gone for good. But Tia continued to have awful, frustrating symptoms. Clearly the avoidance was not helping, which is why she needed therapy … and it was daunting for her.

Another diagnostic criterion for PTSD is that *negative thoughts or mood* must be present in at least two ways. Possible ways for this to be evident include trouble with remembering the event, negative beliefs about self or others (such as "I can't trust anyone ever again"), ongoing negative emotions, decreased interest in activities, feeling detached from others, and the inability to experience positive feelings. Other than not being able to clearly remember the event, Tia experienced all of these. She blamed herself, she was depressed, and she had no interest in activities or people. As a result, she struggled with guilt about not being as active and involved with her children as she would like. She wanted to go to their basketball games but couldn't force herself to sit in the gym; she was afraid to drive on the freeway, so she "lost" the sign-up sheet to chaperone a field trip. These were regular occurrences, and her children were becoming frustrated. They knew about her trauma, although they hadn't been home when it had happened and had no idea their mother had been abused for so many years, but they didn't quite understand Tia's struggle with negative thoughts and feelings.

The final criterion for PTSD, in addition to the symptoms lasting more than a month and causing significant distress or impairment, is *alteration in arousal.* This can include anger, self-destructive behaviors, hyper-vigilance (increased awareness of surroundings), exaggerated startle response, difficulty concentrating, or problems with sleep. At least two of these must be present, and Tia dealt with them all. Because she frequently had nightmares, she did not like to sleep and rarely got more than five hours on any given night. She was hyper-aware of her surroundings to the point of constantly being anxious and alert. Attending church was very difficult for Tia for many reasons, one being that the pews in the sanctuary were situated such that parishioners sat with their backs to the door—an extremely distressing setting for Tia.

The diagnostic criteria are fairly clear, and Tia met them all. Still, the question remains: Why did Tia develop PTSD when many others don't? In other words, what leads one, and not others, to develop PTSD? We tend to think intuitively that the development of PTSD is based on how "bad" the trauma is. And, clearly, Tia went through an intense and horrific series of events. But, believe it or not, the development of PTSD is not related to the severity of the trauma. A number of related theories exist as to why an individual develops PTSD, but one important aspect of this includes influencing factors of PTSD.

What an individual experiences before, during, and after a trauma largely influences the outcome. Tia did not have a strong support system. Her only family was comprised of her adolescent children, and she didn't have a community of trusted friends to rely on for help or to be there for her. This made her recovery even more difficult. Needless to say, developing trust with a therapist proved to be a long-lasting challenge as well. In spite of Tia's resistance to therapy, professional help was imperative for her healing, and certainly is for most who have a PTSD diagnosis. You might be wondering what makes a person susceptible to developing PTSD in the first place. Next, we'll look at the risk factors for this disorder to arise.

RISK FACTORS FOR PTSD

There are three stages of risk factors for the development of PTSD: pre-event (before the trauma), event (during the trauma), and post-event (following the trauma). In other words, there are characteristics, circumstances, and personality traits that contribute to whether PTSD comes about for an individual after experiencing trauma. In this section, we'll look at each one. It's important to note that someone may not fit into any of these and still suffer as a result of trauma.

Pre-event Risk Factors

Of particular interest to those reading this book may be that being female increases the risk of the development of PTSD. This is well established in the trauma field.[2] Other pre-event risk factors for developing PTSD include repeated exposures to trauma such as sexual abuse, physical abuse, or domestic violence.[3] Additionally, Raabe and Spengler report that those who have experienced abuse or mistreatment as children are more likely to be exposed to trauma as an adult and are more likely to develop PTSD as an adult.[4]

Event Risk Factors

For women who have experienced rape, a number of event factors increase their risk of developing PTSD. According to Moller, et al., some of these factors, including being injured, being forced into multiple sexual acts, and being assaulted by more than one person, increase this risk.[5] Level of exposure to a traumatic event may also increase the risk of developing PTSD.[6]

Post-event Risk Factors

Finally, after a traumatic event, lack of social support increases the risk of developing PTSD.[7] In fact, according to this same research, social support is so important that it has been determined to be associated with a lower rate of PTSD! There are other factors to consider as well. For example, does the individual have physical injuries related to the trauma? Does the individual have healthy coping skills? Is the individual able to return to a sense of normalcy after the event (such as their job, their home, etc.)? There is a lot to consider when exploring what increases the risk for one person to develop PTSD over another.

When I was in my late teens, the thought of seeking any kind of help after my surgery never even occurred to me. Now, because I've seen remarkable benefits for those suffering with PTSD as a result of different professional approaches and organizations, I encourage anyone struggling with overwhelming or prolonged symptoms (whether meeting criteria for PTSD or not) to consider any of the various treatment options below. If one doesn't seem to help, I hope you'll try another.

TREATMENT OPTIONS

Psychoeducation is the process of learning about trauma, its impact, and what you can do to work through the symptoms. Psychoeducation is usually a part of therapy but is not actual psychotherapy in and of itself. It is incredibly important to understand what you are dealing with in order to be best prepared *to* deal with it, and psychoeducation does that for you. Not only that, but your family members can also receive education about the way your experiences have had an impact on you, which may help them understand your reaction to trauma and become a better support for you. Psychoeducation will be a part of *all* the options I'll describe in this chapter.

Social or peer support groups can be so helpful. Think of Alcoholics Anonymous but for people who have experienced specific and difficult life events. You know they exist, but did you know they exist for *you*? Support groups are available for those with cancer, those who have lost a loved one to suicide, those who have gone through a divorce, and more. Psychiatrist Irvin Yalom identified and defined eleven curative factors of group therapy. Universality is one of these factors. This means that when people come to a group, they start to recognize they are not the only person experiencing what they are facing. Knowing your problems are not unique and that others have not only experienced similar events, but they experience similar thoughts, feelings, and behaviors, can provide a sense of relief and hope.

Group members can learn a lot from one another, they can help one another, and they can see the improvement that other people experience, which can provide hope. The ability to release long-held emotions in a group of people who can understand (aka *catharsis*) is one more curative factor. There are others, but this gives you an idea of some of the most pertinent. You can find social or peer support groups in your community through a simple Internet search or by calling a local therapist.

Cognitive processing therapy (CPT) is an evidence-based form (meaning research has shown its effectiveness) of therapy that can be offered in individual or group formats. It is a twelve-week program where you go weekly for about an hour to work on your trauma with a therapist. CPT involves processing your experience by writing about it, speaking about it, and addressing the thoughts you have about the trauma that keep you *stuck*. In other words, this form of therapy helps you to work through the negative thoughts that keep running through your mind and lead to negative feelings and behaviors. For example, someone might think, *God doesn't love me because He let something bad happen to me.* This thought might lead this person to feel sad, angry, confused, or any number of other emotions. Through CPT, an individual in this position could work through this belief by challenging it with the help of a therapist. CPT is also helpful at increasing trust, safety, intimacy, and more.

Prolonged exposure (PE) is another evidence-based form of therapy that calls for individuals with PTSD to meet weekly for ninety minutes with a licensed therapist, in order to process through the traumatic event by writing and speaking about it in-depth. You may be asking yourself, "Why would I ever want to *talk* about this terrible thing that happened to me?" I know it's tough, but many people feel much better as a result of going through the challenging but rewarding process of therapy. The good news in all of this is that there is a form of therapy that can help you regardless of how much or how little you wish to talk about the trauma. It's more important to address the impact it has had on you rather than the trauma itself.

Eye movement desensitization and reprocessing (EMDR) is a third evidence-based form of therapy that is used for the treatment of PTSD. According to the National Center for PTSD website, where you can learn more about all three of these PTSD therapy options, "While thinking of or talking about your memories, you'll focus on other stimuli like eye movements, hand taps, and sounds."[8] While eye movement desensitization and reprocessing are still being studied, substantial evidence suggests its effectiveness at reducing PTSD symptoms. It has also been used in group formats with children and adults who have struggled with trauma.[9] EMDR is definitely a treatment worth looking into and considering if you are in need of professional help.

Psychotropic medications can also be helpful in the management of symptoms, such as depression, anxiety, and nightmares, associated with PTSD. Of course, medications, including mental health medications, should be taken only upon discussion and agreement with your health-care provider. When discussing medications, it's important to keep in mind their limitations. For example, antidepressants have been demonstrated to be effective for about one-third of the people who take them, which means most people do not benefit from taking them.[10] In fact, the federal drug administration (FDA) has approved only two medications for the treatment of PTSD. That being said, some other medications are used to treat specific concerns that people who experience trauma have, even if the person does not develop PTSD as a result of the trauma. If you truly need them, medications can be helpful, but I always recommend psychotherapy in conjunction with medication.

For Tia, finding a path to health took several tries before she was finally able to commit to regular psychotherapy sessions. It wasn't easy, and when things got challenging, she avoided treatment. She frequently canceled appointments and took time off from counseling, but would always return. The same may be true for you. Perhaps you've suffered from PTSD for so long, you're not sure what life would be like without it. Maybe it's even become your "frenemy"—a friend only in that you're used to it, but also your mortal enemy because it never stops weighing you down. For Tia, the cycle of starting and stopping therapy went on and on until she got to that "enough is enough" point and decided to give psychotherapy her all. When she committed to it, she found counseling extremely helpful and her negative symptoms decreased. The same can be true for you.

WHAT WAS NOAH THINKING?

You know the Bible story of Noah. In Noah's day, humanity had become so vile that God's heart was broken and filled with grief over His creation's choices. So, God destroyed every living thing except Noah, his family, and two of each animal. Essentially, God started over but still made a way for humankind, as well as for the animals He so lovingly created, to carry on. Yet humans continued to sin. I don't know if the world is any better or any worse than it was on the day of the great flood, but I do know this: Jesus has not yet returned for a reason. And throughout the book of Revelation, He calls us to stand firm until that day comes. He calls us to overcome and to do His will regardless of what we're faced with. These words are sometimes agonizing to hear when something bad has happened and we cry out, "Even so, come, Lord Jesus!" Standing firm takes time and lots of hard, painstaking work. Even when the diagnosis isn't PTSD, tackling any emotional or behavioral health concerns is challenging. It was for Tia. Central to living a life of faith is leaning in and clinging to what Jesus says, and not what our own minds or the world around us says.

What was Noah feeling during the harrowing times in his life? If I were him, I would have been a bit shaky, distraught—terrified even. I'm sure he had many, many questions and concerns, not knowing what was going to happen or what the end result would be. Yet, despite everything going on outside of him and inside of him, he remained faithful to God. While it's much easier said than done, and pat answers aren't the intention of this book, it *is* possible to trust God and rest in Him even while the storm rages. We'll spend some time focusing on how to tackle that together in the chapters ahead.

CHAPTER 5

IT'S NOT JUST ABOUT PTSD

"God is our refuge and strength, an ever-present help in trouble."

Psalm 46:1

Fear, anxiety, and depression are just a few emotional ways people might respond to a traumatic event. It is important to recognize these and own them in order to change one's response and leave these negative emotions behind.

Groggy from the morphine, but not completely out of it, I let the surgeon know I had two questions for him. The first question, "Have you done this before?" garnered some chuckles from everyone in the room (which was fairly crowded with my parents, friends, and nurses). The surgeon smiled and assured me he had. Still not ready to trust him, I doubled down and asked, "Do you know my father is a lawyer?"

The laughs at my follow-up question were even louder. Everyone thought it was the medication talking, but I had every intention of asking those questions before I was wheeled into surgery that day. I needed some reassurance that the surgeon knew what he was doing and would do the best job he possibly could. I figured a little healthy fear of a lawsuit would work in my favor.

Fortunately, I didn't develop ASD or PTSD as a result of my lifesaving surgery, but that doesn't mean this difficult experience didn't leave a lasting impact. As mentioned in chapter 2, I continued to experience ongoing anxiety and seasons of worry because of that unexpected and fearful event. I don't recall having many negative emotions in the first few weeks after surgery. I was relieved to have survived and was excited about a new svelte figure (and shopping for new clothes!). I took the semester off of school, and after a few weeks, I was working again full time.

All in all, I was doing well. But, then, I had a pretty serious health scare. Soon I started noticing every single bodily sensation. *Noticing* became *obsessing*: a headache, an upset stomach, a muscle spasm—worry began to plague my mind. What *else* might go wrong with me? What *else* might I have to go through? What if *this time* I didn't survive? I hate to admit it, but there is still a twinge of that fear residing in me—even though my surgery trauma is more than fifteen years in my past. As a result, it's easy for me to become upset if I get sick. I'm not talking about getting upset over a cold, but when a pain shows up and it's not immediately clear what is wrong, or if the illness lingers, I find myself feeling unraveled and consumed with "what ifs."

For example, in 2007, I went through several months of daily nausea and almost daily vomiting—enough to make anyone concerned, right? I wasn't pregnant, wasn't struggling with bulimia, and the doctors could not figure out *what* was wrong, which made me even more wobbly and insecure about my health. Was this all in my head? Finally, one test revealed it could be my gallbladder. While the surgeon wasn't convinced of the culprit, she recommended removal—I recall her saying that even if the issue wasn't my gallbladder, it wouldn't hurt to have it removed. (For me, that wasn't exactly true.) Thankfully, while getting used to not having a gallbladder is no fun, the surgery did end the nausea and vomiting. Now that you know the good outcome, let me back up.

The physical symptoms of nausea (not only the queasy, sweaty feeling, but the "death-warmed-over," muscles-aching, head-achy, feverish feeling) are similar to the physical symptoms of anxiety. As a result, it can be difficult to tell which one is making its presence known. For me, I definitely had the former, and sometimes the latter. But during this particular illness, my symptoms were more emotional than physical. I spent a lot of time focused on what was wrong with me—and researching on the Internet (and self-diagnosing, of course). It is natural for anyone to be concerned or even focused on a health concern they are facing, but the symptoms were heightened and more complicated because my nausea *triggered reminders* of my lifesaving surgery. These few months were a real struggle. I was afraid.

Can you relate? Cancer survivors often feel "cancer-free" only until the next checkup, or until the next lump or ache. "Free" can be a misnomer. You know this isn't PTSD, but you can still relate. You see yourself in this same boat. The waves are rocking the boat so hard that seasickness comes crashing in. You're flailing around in the stormy dark unable to find the anchor. You cry out. Something has to give or you might just sink or be washed away. Fear, anxiety, and depression are just a few emotional ways people might respond to a traumatic event. Our physical bodies do not feel safe. Maybe you're dealing with this even now. Jesus makes some claims that maybe we're not altogether too sure about. We know the Bible stories about Jesus calming the sea, but will He calm this one?

PEACE OF GOD

Remember how Jesus told His followers they would have trouble? Okay, you've got that part down pat. Yeah, you know trouble. But what about the rest of the verse? The part about Jesus overcoming the world (John 16:33)? What about where He says He came to give us peace? This is a core part of who Jesus is and what He came to do.

Jesus said, "Peace I leave with you; my peace I give you. I do not give to you as the world gives. Do not let your hearts be troubled and do not be afraid" (John 14:27). I did a word study of the Greek used here in John 14:27, and though the original word translates to "peace" in the English language, it's believed that this word (*éirenén*) can mean "welfare." God is concerned about our entire well-being. Let's take a look together at Ephesians 2:14–18 and consider how this passage relates to finding peace:

For he himself is our peace, who has made the two groups one and has destroyed the barrier, the dividing wall of hostility, by setting aside in his flesh the law with its commands and regulations. His purpose was to create in himself one new humanity out of the two, thus making peace, and in one body to reconcile both of them to God through the cross, by which he put to death their hostility. *He came and preached peace to you who were far away and peace to those who were near.* For through him we both have access to the Father by one Spirit.

Whether you feel near or far away, peace and well-being are what God intends for you. Reread the very first words of verse 14: "Jesus is our peace."

Christ's very essence is peace.

God tells us that His peace surpasses all our thoughts, ruminations, and logic through His Son, Jesus. Read the words of Philippians 4:7: "And the peace of God, which transcends all understanding, will guard your hearts and your minds in Christ Jesus." Have you ever thought about that? That God has sent us our own guard? Not just over our general abstract existence, but the peace that comes from Him protects literally our hearts and *minds*. I get the image of a little guard with the words "Peace of God" written on the back of his uniform, marching between my heart and mind to protect me in the name of Jesus. We don't understand this type of around-the-clock peace because it is beyond the scope of our limited understanding that we could live in a world so pitted with turmoil and strife and still find peace. That we could experience trauma, stress, and overwhelming life events and still rest easy in the Father's arms. God protects, shields, guards, and keeps our souls safe in peace, so we don't have to be afraid. Through Jesus, this peace can be present with us no matter what is going on inside of us or all around us. I'll say more on this as we move along.

WHY ARE YOU SO AFRAID?

We have access to a fathomless sea of resources: community, the Internet, therapists, and more. But eventually each of us will come to a point when we must ask, "Who or what is my ultimate voice of authority? Is God who God says He is? Can I trust God to do what God says He will do? Do I believe? Will I see the world and my story through my point of view, or dare I consider seeing through a different set of lenses—from God's point of view? Can I believe in this kind of peace?"

Matthew 8 tells about the time Jesus was with His disciples on a boat when a storm came up on the Sea of Galilee. The disciples were filled with fear, grabbing buckets and ropes, holding on for dear life as the boat heaved and lurched on the swelling waves. "Where is He?" they yelled while crawling along toward where they last saw Jesus. Then Jesus calmed the storm with one single rebuke. It was completely calm, the Bible says. The men were amazed and asked, "What kind of man is this? Even the wind and waves obey him!" (Matthew 8:27).

What strikes me the most about this story is that Jesus asked His disciples the strangest question in this circumstance, "You of little faith, why are you so afraid?" Seriously? Quite obviously anyone would be freaking out about the very real possibility of being tossed overboard and drowned at sea. So what was Jesus getting at? Although His followers were with Jesus in the flesh, they were being called out for a lack of trust and for being afraid while in the presence of "God, Mighty Creator" (*Elohim*) of both the wind and the sea. I believe this has a couple of simple but important implications for us when we face trials in life.

First, God who created all things and is sovereign over all, calls us to put our faith in Him alone. Not in human beings. Not in government or world leaders. And certainly not in the weather. Some people live in really grave circumstances on a day-to-day basis and still live full and abundant lives. Their faces radiate joy. While it is easier said than done, living by faith cannot be based on our circumstances. External things change, but Jesus doesn't.

Second, we have no need to be afraid. Jesus talks a lot about not being afraid. If you back up a couple of chapters from Jesus calming the storm, He devotes Matthew 6:25–34 to instructing us not to worry. He tells us that we don't need to worry about our lives because God will take care of all the details. Even when life doesn't go as planned, and even when life gets really rough, worrying does not add a single moment to our lives. (For more on worry, see chapter 13.)

Our job is to stop denying the terrifying or distressing event(s), recognize our emotions, own them, and then begin leaning into the truth and authority of God, who holds the blueprints for our well-being. Only then can we begin to leave negative emotions behind. This is not a quick fix, but with time and practice, the symptoms of trauma can begin to fade.

A few chapters later in Matthew 14, we find the disciples again setting sail, only this time without Jesus. They went on ahead without Jesus so He could spend time alone in prayer. In the black of night, when the disciples were already a long way from shore, the wind kicked up and the waves were again "buffeting the boat." (Not fun! They must have been furious with Jesus for not being there when they needed Him.) When Jesus, who didn't seem to be in any hurry, was ready to go out to the disciples on the boat, He took the shortest route and walked across the water.

We've all seen bizarre things when we're terrified, and the disciples were sure they were seeing a ghost. "Lord, if it's you," Peter cried out, "tell me to come to you on the water."

"'Come,' he said" (Matthew 14:29).

Jesus was who He said He was. Peter, by keeping his eyes on Jesus, was able to walk on the water. "But when he saw the wind, he was afraid and, beginning to sink, cried out, 'Lord, save me!'" (Matthew 14:30). Immediately, Jesus reached out His hand and caught hold of him.

Once again, Jesus called Peter out for his lack of faith. Jesus, who had just spent time with His Father in prayer, must have wondered why Peter was still so blind to the truth of Peace. Jesus sees us, comes to us, calls to us, catches us. But He also asks us to trust

Him. "Why did you doubt?" Jesus asked. We really have only two choices, to trust God or live in sinking turmoil.

If you'll allow Jesus to be your peace, He will pull you out of sinking turmoil. Then you can begin to know Him as your healing and hope.

CHAPTER 6

MORE THAN A BAND-AID: HOPE AND HEALING START HERE

"Come to me, all who are weary and
burdened, and I will give you rest.
Take my yoke upon you and learn from me,
for I am gentle and humble in heart,
and you will find rest for your souls."

Matthew 11:28–29

Jesus is our Peace in times of tsunami-sized troubles, but do you ever wonder about what hope we have for healing from trauma and life's overwhelming trials? There is hope and healing for those who are in Christ. Developing a daily dependence on God and getting to know the Holy Spirit as our counselor will help us eventually replace our negative, self-sabotaging thoughts and behaviors.

We were all on our feet swaying as the all-girl band led us in the beautiful melodic chorus: *I need you, oh I need you. Every hour I need you.*[1] Tears streamed down my cheeks as I sang along with my eyes closed and hands raised. I was still recovering from a brief but difficult illness, and my desire for God was more apparent and urgent than it had been in a while. Sadly, I don't always recognize my desperate need for God during the good times. When it comes to being friends with Jesus, I can be a bit of a user. It seems that it's only during the storms in life that I understand how much I need Him. I pray more, read the Scriptures more, and worship Him more during times of trial.

A few months prior to this soul-filling time of worship, I was driving down the road, waiting on a call from my doctor's office. Barely able to keep my head up, but needing to make the trip, I listened to Michael O'Brien praise songs the whole time. It's what I needed, y'all. *I was afraid.* Not knowing what was wrong with me or what the treatment would be, I needed the reassurance that God was good. That He loved me with an everlasting love. That if He sent His only Son to die in my place for my sins, of course He loved me enough to hold me close, to keep me safe, through an illness—through this particular illness—regardless of the outcome. This is why spending time with Jesus is so important. We *all* need to be pulled into the eternal embrace. And worship songs sure did help me survive during times when I thought I might be losing my mind.

WHO *IS* THIS PERSON?

For those who've suffered great stress or trauma, personality changes—or what seem to be—are not uncommon following a traumatic event. In reality, these are not personality changes so much as they are modifications in behavior based on the experience. Sometimes surprising responses are simply coping skills, even when negative. Reactions can usually be justified. They can also wreck your family. You can choose to rein these behaviors in. The pull of addiction and escape is strong, but God's love is stronger. The next several chapters offer practical counseling tips for addressing problematic behaviors, thoughts, and feelings, but let's first focus on the best counselor of all.

Not long before the gallbladder debacle began, I had applied to a PhD program. This was a major step because I had spent months (and months) researching programs. I was so excited to find a program that I knew would be the perfect fit for me. Isn't it interesting how the Lord works? I was in a bookstore one day and ran into a girl I had not seen since high school. We greeted each other and got to chatting when I asked her what she was up to these days. She shared she was about to graduate from Regent University. Had I heard of it? she asked. I hadn't, so I decided to look it up as soon as I got home. Imagine my surprise when I discovered a PhD program that seemed just the right fit. Before I knew it, I was applying.

When it was time for my interview, I had already been dealing with the nausea and vomiting resulting from my gallbladder problem for weeks. I hated to miss the interview when the program meant so much to me. I believed God was calling me to it, so my husband and in-laws drove me the two states away to the university. You never forget the moment your mother-in-law yells, "Pull over!" and your husband almost loses control of the vehicle while those in the car think you're choking. Nope, no need for the Heimlich; just dry heaving. Sigh.

Anyway, I barely made it to the chapel on campus. There I saw a prayer book, and as I knelt at the front of that little chapel, I wrote in the book my plea for God to hear me, specifically, that I would return to that site completely healed. While I did have to defer enrollment for a year, when I finally made it back and was again able to visit the chapel, I found my original prayer and made a note that my prayer had been answered in a beautiful way. I was healed!

I share this story with you not to say that we will be *cured* from physical or emotional hurt, because I personally cannot make that promise. Rather, I tell you this story to say that we can be *healed and held safe*. God is always listening and responding and drawing near. He knows our pain and wants us to know of His presence, even while desiring or begging that our troubles be taken from us. God has not only sustained me throughout the physically and emotionally difficult journeys; God has given me the strength to keep going. Day in, day out, with hope each hour, as well as for the future. This is a form of healing.

IN THE "WAR ROOM" WITH JESUS

Have you seen the movie *War Room*? It's a 2015 film starring Priscilla Shirer. Her character, Elizabeth, meets an older woman named Miss Clara who has a prayer closet in her house. The movie is all about the power of prayer and the amazing blessing of keeping track of prayer requests, which I invite you to do for yourself. Each day we walk with Jesus, we can lean into His great love and learn more about what it means to pray without ceasing (1 Thessalonians 5:17). We can wake up in the morning and talk to God throughout the day, listening to His words of wisdom and prompting of great love in the pages of Scripture. We might pause and then chat a little more. Sometimes, we might cry and argue. We can lament and complain. We can ask for forgiveness and give thanks. And when our nights are long and lonely, we can talk to God then too.

Journaling is extremely therapeutic and often recommended by mental health professionals. For me, I'm able to process what I am experiencing by writing out what I'm dealing with, what I'm thinking, and how I'm feeling. I also keep track of prayer requests and the answers to my prayers. God always answers our prayers. He may not answer them in the timing or in the way that we want, but He does always answer. I can't say I understand how prayer works, but I do believe in the power of prayer, and looking back over the pages of my journal reminds me of this. I also love that journaling helps me see how present Jesus is in the midst of some of life's most confusing and trying moments and how my emotion at the time, though legitimate, did not dictate the outcome.

While you may not be completely relieved of suffering, you can experience a decrease in symptoms and an increase in faith through prayer. And, really, even if symptoms don't decrease, God can provide the strength to face the challenges of each day. How have you seen prayer work in your life and in the lives of others? When you doubt prayer (and you will!), meditate on and remember how you have seen prayer work in the past. God still answers prayers!

"Hope is not merely the optimistic view that somehow everything will turn out all right in the end if everyone just does as we do. Hope is the more rugged, the more muscular view that even if things don't turn out all right and aren't all right, we endure through and beyond the times that disappoint or threaten to destroy us."[2]

Peter Gomes, *The Scandalous Gospel of Jesus*

What hope do we have for healing? For those who are in Christ Jesus, each day we journey with Him who suffers with us and for us, and as our relationship grows more trusting, we discover a daily dependence on God. Rather than just a means to an end, God *is* the hope we seek; He is our peace and safety, our ever-present—our daily, hourly, minute-by-minute—help. The Holy Spirit, our counselor, guides and teaches us how to replace negative, self-sabotaging thoughts and behaviors. Ultimately, we know our Jesus as redeemer of our everyday suffering, and this changes everything. One day we will wake up knowing how deeply loved we are.

If you wrestle with the recurrent thought of *I can't take it anymore*, you are not alone. God is with you, even if you do not feel

His presence right now. He is the God who sees (*Jehovah El Roi*), the God who helps (*Jehovah Ezer*), and the God who heals (*Jehovah Rapha*). God wants to help you reclaim who He has created and called you to be.

In the next section of the book, Reclaiming Me, we'll look at some ways that trauma, stress, and overwhelming life events affect our ability to be who we are designed to be. With a focus on frustration and facing the past, this section will help hone your ability to manage thoughts and feelings that are unproductive or harmful and point you back to the truth. Get ready to take off the masks you've been hiding behind and let the world see who you really are. It's not as scary as it sounds when we remember that we are who God says we are.

PART II

RECLAIMING ME

"Trials teach us what we are;
they dig up the soil,
and let us see what we are made of."

Charles Spurgeon

CHAPTER 7

DEALING WITH A TOUGH PAST

"If the Son sets you free, you will be free indeed."

John 8:36

This chapter will help you explore how your upbringing might play a role in the difficulty of managing your emotions today. Consider how various emotions were expressed by your parents or those who raised you, how you were disciplined, and what messages you received about women and emotions. We'll begin looking at the impact the past has on the present and how you can find freedom from a tough past.

RACHEL'S STORY

Now a successful businesswoman, Rachel wasn't always sure she was even going to survive. Born to a mother she'd never met because of a serious mental illness, and raised by a stepmother who physically abused her while her father turned a blind eye, she did not have a great start in life. Rachel shared with me that though she knew almost nothing about God, she trusted someone bigger than herself—and bigger than the abuse she routinely experienced. While she not only survived and is fortunate to thrive now in life, she still experiences the emotional ramifications of a traumatic past. As a result, Rachel struggles with setting healthy boundaries in her relationships. Sometimes she gets too close too soon. Other times she withdraws and avoids. Rachel works hard to overcome the impact of her rocky childhood, but it's tough going.

Dealing with the lingering results of a difficult childhood isn't relegated to pain suffered at the hands of one's family of origin. Managing emotional pain and other negative consequences may stem from other childhood traumas. School shootings, human trafficking (outside the home), and childhood cancer are examples of non-family-related experiences that carry far-reaching impact for a child. The same is true for house fires, car accidents, and natural disasters. And unfortunately, the list goes on and on. Countless events or circumstances experienced as a child can affect one's adulthood. **The reality is that our past, our whole past, affects our present.** Memories of these types of events can lead to those overwhelming feelings that we don't know what to do with in the present.

Of course, not all traumatic, stressful, or overwhelming life events happen in childhood; we've mentioned experiences faced by adult women. Still, we recognize that **sometimes reclaiming sanity**

means going back to childhood, where defense mechanisms and coping skills are learned. If you've been in an environment wherein defense mechanisms were used to protect yourself, or you were not able to learn healthy coping skills, you are likely to struggle with current stressful events. You may be familiar with commonly known and frequently used defense mechanisms such as denial and displacement.

Denial is when your heart and mind aren't ready to accept the truth or reality of a situation. Like Rachel, you might tell yourself that you deserved the physical abuse you suffered at the hands of your stepmother because you didn't behave well enough. You rationalize (another defense mechanism) that she was doing the best she could, that her behavior wasn't abuse because she loved you and did it because she believed it was good discipline, and that your father would have stopped it if he had known what was going on.

Displacement, on the other hand, is when negative emotions or behaviors are channeled *not* toward the object or person you are actually upset with, but toward someone safer. Staying with Rachel's story, instead of getting angry at your stepmother for the abuse, perhaps you lash out in anger toward your sister, who was not abused. Instead of being angry with the abusive person and risking further abuse, you become angry with someone who is weaker because they are safer.

When looking at your past, it's important to explore what coping skills and defense mechanisms you were exposed to and taught, and how you are using them today. It's not too late to change.[1]

YOUR FAMILY OF ORIGIN

In order to understand the emotions confronting you in the present, examining your past is a necessity. To start with, it may be important to revisit the way you were raised. **Often, the way emotions were expressed in your family of origin (that is, the family you grew up with) affects the way you express emotions today.** We won't dive into the specific events you experienced as a child, but you are encouraged to begin exploring your childhood.

The following exercise will ask you to think about the family you grew up in, how you were disciplined, the messages you received about women and men, etc. Think carefully about these as you answer, reflecting on how this affects you today. You may start to notice patterns of behavior you would like to change. If you find these memories are too painful for you to deal with, this could be an indicator that you may benefit from meeting with a mental health professional.

Please answer the following questions about the family in which you grew up.[2]

1. Describe the family you grew up with. Include your parents/guardians, siblings, and anyone else who lived with you at any point during your childhood.

_____

_____

_____

_____

2. How were emotions expressed in your family while you were growing up? Think about positive, negative, and neutral emotions.

_____

_____

_____

_____

3. How were you disciplined? If you have children in your life, do you discipline similarly or differently? In what ways?

_____

_____

_____

_____

4. What messages did you receive about how women should behave? What did you think about those messages? How are those messages still present in your thinking today?

_____

_____

_____

_____

5. Do you have any unresolved feelings about your childhood? If so, describe them here.

_____

_____

_____

6. As a result of this exercise, what have you learned about the impact the past may be having on your present?

_____

_____

_____

_____

Now that you've taken some time to think about your family of origin, it may be more apparent that your upbringing and any traumatic events that might have taken place prior to now can continue to strike blows against you today and impede your recovery if they are not sufficiently dealt with. It's possible this exercise brought up some memories and feelings that are tough to cope with. Again, it may be a good idea to work with a mental health professional who can help you process through these experiences more thoroughly.

PRAYER BREAKS CHAINS WITH THE PAST

In Mark 9, Jesus encountered a boy possessed by a demon. Jesus was able to do what His disciples could not: rid the boy of the demon. The disciples asked Jesus why they were unable to drive the demon out. In verse 29, Jesus responded in this way: "This kind can come out only by prayer." As a result of prayer, Jesus was able to do what seemed to be impossible.

I encourage you to pray also, specifically about those hurtful memories from your past that haunt you. Kind of like demons, it may seem that the haunting experiences from a tough past will never go away. You may be questioning how you can ever "get over" your past. The fact is that there is nothing we can do to change the past. Yet, there is a lot we can do about the way we react to the reminders of the past while living fully in the present and leaning into the future.

Like King David, who experienced a war-torn life and is believed to have suffered from PTSD, you can cry out the words of the psalms he wrote and, undoubtedly, prayed over and over. David often began his prayers with anger and lashing out and asking why, but ended them by praising the Lord. "It is crucial for us to remember that although the Psalms begin with our internal world," advised authors Dan Allender and Tremper Longman, "they don't allow us to dwell there, fixated on our problems and dark emotions … the Psalter is a book of worship, driving us to God by insisting that we look to Him in the midst of our pain."[3] We can choose sanity, and prayer is integral to that choice.

NANCY'S STORY

Despite an abusive childhood, Nancy exuded joy. She still needed help from time to time to get a refresher on what she had learned after years of therapy to recover from the sexual abuse she experienced at the hands of her father. But she had recovered sufficiently to where she enjoyed life again. She had suffered as a result of her past far too long and decided she would not give any more time to anger, sadness, and worry over a past she couldn't change. For

Nancy, faith was a major part of her recovery. Her pain could only be released through prayer. She spent a lot of time crying out to God for healing, and while she still faced some negative thoughts and feelings from time to time, she was able to focus on her present life rather than her destructive past.

What made her journey so challenging was that her abuse came from the very hands that were designed to love and protect her most. When children are abused or neglected by their caregivers, the scars run deep and last a long time. Nancy was older by the time we met. Her husband had passed away and her children had long since become adults. An empty nester who lived alone, she still had to work extra hard to deter upsetting memories of serious trauma from the past and the resulting negative consequences from creeping into her mind. She had also experienced the sweetness of reprieve from her emotional pain. Each day she intentionally chose which memories she would keep and which she would release through a mindfulness approach to her thinking. (More on that later!)

Nancy refused to allow her abusive father to have continued control over her, and she came to rely on *Abba*, her heavenly Father, for the love and support she needed and desired. Of course, it would be easier to give in to anger, bitterness, and depression; it takes great strength to not let these undeserved emotions consume you, but it is possible. You can stop searching for that *one thing* that will make it all go away. While you may not experience 100 percent relief from your pain, you can reclaim sanity, clarity, and peace—even from the tragedies that have plagued you from childhood. And you can begin now to experience a decrease in pain after whatever trauma, stress, or overwhelming life events you've been through.

As I've already stated, the process of recovery is not easy, but it is worth it. Instead of being a prisoner to your past, you can learn to cope with it in healthy ways. Take a look at what the Bible has to say on this topic.

1. God gives us the instructions and guidance we need to cope with a difficult past. Read Isaiah 43:18–19. How do these verses speak to you regarding your past and coping with any difficulties from it?

_____

_____

_____

_____

2. Read the book of Philippians. (It's only about three pages long.) Pull out at least one verse that you can cling to during times when you feel overwhelmed by your past hurts. Write it down below and again on an index card that you can carry with you.

_____

_____

_____

_____

Bible scholars believe they know precisely which valley King David was writing about when he penned his most beloved psalm, twenty-three. David was a real person who not only suffered grave consequences as a result of his own sin, but had been sinned against as well. Like the rest of us, the psalmist knew dark valleys where robbers and thieves hid. Regardless of your past, may you, like David, boldly proclaim the words of the twenty-third psalm: "Yea, though I walk through the darkest valley, I will fear no evil for you are with me … You prepare a table before me in the presence of my enemies." Make this your declaration, regardless of your past, now and forevermore.

"Surely goodness and mercy shall follow me all the days of my life."

CHAPTER 8

FACES OF FRUSTRATION

*"We demolish arguments and every pretension that sets
itself up against the knowledge of God, and we take
captive every thought to make it obedient to Christ."*

2 Corinthians 10:5

*This chapter explores four "faces" (or causes) of frustration or anger:
entitlement, power (or control), habit, and masking other emotions.
Many consequences are experienced as a result of being out of control
with these emotions. While these feelings are not sinful or wrong, they
can become a problem if we allow them to consume us and dictate
who we are at the core. Facing these frustrations mindfully involves
understanding the faces of frustration.*

I'd only *tried* to put them on … only once, and I'd saved the
receipt, but the saleswoman at the department store *still* refused
my Spanx return. Although I followed the sizing on the back

of the package, the wonder garment that was about the size of newborn's bloomers simply would not fit—any higher than my knees. Sigh. I'd had big hopes but just could *not* make the magical bottom-thigh, tummy-tucking minimizers work.

I thought I was following the return policy (after all, they'd never been worn), but apparently, there was no return policy, and the salesclerk refused to see my point of view. When she became rude, I became, ahem, *very* frustrated. As in, I made a scene—you know the kind. I raised my voice and practically stomped my feet while demanding to have my way—all the while embarrassing my husband, Nick, who wasn't at all thrilled at being in the lingerie department to begin with.

My fury wasn't even about the cost—hello! You know the price of these little nude-colored dream stealers—it was about the principle, and failed promises. Fortunately, I ended up negotiating a gift card from the store manager, so you might say that all ended well. However, the painful truth was that the end result might have been the same had I stayed calm, *and* Nick wouldn't now have a twitch every time we walk past that department store. I would have left the store feeling fine instead of embarrassed and exasperated. And the salesclerk's day might have been a little more peaceful as well.

Everyone gets frustrated, irritated, even angry from time to time. Even *Christian* women. And those who have been through trauma, overwhelming life events, or excessive stress tend to become frustrated, irritated, or angry more frequently—sometimes without even knowing why. If this describes you, and if you are like many other Christian women, you feel bad about yourself every time you "lose it." While what we are experiencing is well within the range of typical human emotions, the mood swings may be more intense and frequent than they should be, which can result in serious problems. You may even feel as if you've lost yourself to these emotions. But the good news is that you can reclaim yourself and rediscover your best self.

If you fit the description of one who has intense and frequent episodes where frustration gets the better of you; if you have difficulty managing your emotions or their accompanying behaviors; or, if you, like many Christian women, feel terrible about yourself every time you blow up, lash out, or shut down, you are wise to seek help. Good for you for taking the first step by reading this book! Your emotional well-being affects the way you think, feel, and behave.

What about *guilt*? Maybe you have been fighting a losing battle with guilt, which is anger with yourself. "You have violated a belief you have about the way you should think, act or feel and you're mad at yourself for doing so. You may be left with immobilizing regret."[1] Before we go any further, I want you to promise to treat yourself with love, respect, and kindness—and eventually even with forgiveness (we'll talk about that in chapter 14). Women, how can we serve and care for anyone else when we aren't caring for ourselves? Even the airlines remind us to place the oxygen masks on our faces in the event of an emergency before attempting to help our children. You can gain control over your frustrations in order to reduce the negative impact anger has on your life and to experience what Jesus was talking about in John 10:10 when He said He came to give you full and abundant life!

TROUBLING EMOTION

In their book *Cry of the Soul: How Our Emotions Reveal Our Deepest Questions about God*, Dan Allender and Tremper Longman remind us that emotions are a vital part of being in touch with our souls and that by acknowledging emotion rather than denying, we can know the heart of God. Allender and Longman suggest, "Too often we find ourselves caught between the extremes of feeling too much or not at all. We ignore them, fight them, battling as if they are the enemy. But through our emotions (whether positive or negative) we catch a glimpse of the true nature of God."[2]

Is it really possible to learn more about God and grow closer to Him as a result of anger or jealousy? Sure. Whether it be anger, fear, envy and jealousy, shame, abandonment and despair, or holy contempt, each emotion can be righteous or unrighteous, demanding or redemptive, holy or corrupt, dark or divine, stemming from our desire either to be in control or to lean into the heart of God. Let's take an honest look (with grace!), then set about reclaiming our true identity.

All emotions come from God. Yes, even anger. Like the beautiful foods provided by the hand of God for us to eat (think homemade bread just out of the oven and dark chocolate filled with salted caramel), emotions in excess—indulging too frequently or too strongly—are destructive to many areas of life. Emotions left unchecked affect physical health, relationships, and overall emotional well-being. *What are we made of?* Charles Spurgeon suggests that "trials teach us what we are."

Let's take a good look at the four "faces" (or causes) of frustration or anger: entitlement, power (or control), habit, and masking other emotions. Many consequences are experienced as a result of being out of control with these emotions. While these feelings are not sinful or wrong, they can become a problem if we allow them to consume us and dictate who we are at the core. Allender and Longman remind us that to "explore our emotions is not to get rid of the bad ones and replace with good ones, but rather to know God more fully."[3]

THE FOUR FACES OF FRUSTRATION

"The quality that strikes us when looking into the eyes of
a little child is her innocence: her lovely inability to lie or
wear a mask or to be anything other than who she is."
Anthony DeMello

We've discussed many reasons throughout this book for why women get overly frustrated as a result of daily stresses as well as those exacerbated by the residual pain of past trauma, and I'm sure you can think of a few more yourself. Between family, friends, work, church, and life in general, there is plenty of opportunity for our fuses to burn. But what does frustration really indicate? Have you ever wondered if you are *actually* frustrated? What is the likelihood that your irritation is merely masking other underlying thoughts or feelings?

Like putting on makeup to hide the dark circles from sleepless nights, we put on frustration to cover what's really going on. Hearing the truth is not always easy. But truth, spoken in this chapter and throughout, is designed to set you free. Scripture tells us to "speak the truth in love" (Ephesians 4:15), and this is the guideline for our next discussion. Some of the following may make you say "Ouch," but if you want to walk in freedom, here we go!

1. Entitlement

All of us—men, women, children, and especially those of us in developed countries—subscribe to a mistaken belief that we *deserve* certain things in life; and when we aren't allowed these certain things, we get upset. For example, we get hurt, then furious, when we feel disrespected. We get angry when others don't treat us as we believe we should be treated. We get impatient when others don't move on our timetable. We get exasperated when our husbands procrastinate. Or when children misbehave. In the drive-through. In the driveway. We. Get. Frustrated.

If you're like me, you change what you'd *like* to have into what you believe you *must* have; the things you *wish* to have into things you *should* have; what you *hope* to have into what you *ought* to have; and the things you *prefer* into things you are *entitled* to. So, you—okay, we—demand what we want. The problem is that being demanding doesn't mean we get what we want. As the Serenity Prayer states, you have to learn to "accept the things you cannot change." Getting angry over what is unchangeable will not help you. In fact, getting angry can lead to physical, emotional, cognitive, and behavioral consequences. We live in the age of entitlement. Recognizing you are entitled to only taxes and death allows you to feel more gratitude when you do not receive what you want.

One day I was sitting on a plane next to a man who was from an underdeveloped country. He had left his country and in time had made a good living for himself in America. When his children were teenagers, he took them back to his home country to show them what life was like when he was growing up. What startled his kids the most wasn't the lack of material wealth or possessions, but the fact that everyone *seemed so content regardless of how little they had*. Living in a land of plenty leaves us believing we are entitled to what we have and more. But we're not. Rather, we are fortunate and blessed to have what we do.

Do you believe you deserve something you haven't gotten? Take a moment to think about this question—and be totally honest with yourself. Then mentally list a number of things you're thankful for.

2. Control

Do you wish you could control other people? Let's be honest here. Though women are known to be artisans of subtlety with nearly invisible manipulations, little guilt trips, and "sweet" verbal debates, control is a common tactic among us. Most of us want to be in command of everything around us: our homes, our office, our husbands, and our children, just to name a few. However, we forget that there is only so much we can do to govern situations. We forget that God is sovereign. It is simply not wise to manipulate those around us as a means to get them to do what we want. Even if you are only seeking an apology, attempting to force someone to apologize will not improve the relationship.

Do you wish you could change or control someone or something? God does not force obedience, so why do we? Every person on this planet has been granted freedom of choice, and needless to say, many need strong supervision and guidance (especially children); still, this does not mean we have permission to demand control, which usually only results in a battle of wills. If relinquishing power is something you struggle with, I highly recommend Karen Ehman's book *Let. It. Go: How to Stop Running the Show and Start Walking in Faith*.

Do you wish you could change or control someone or something? Consider writing about this honestly in a journal.

3. Habit

I believe God provided anger to be like a flashing indicator light (like in the dashboard of your car) that something is not right. But if the light flashes continually, it no longer serves its original purpose. If the check-engine light never goes off, you don't know when to check the engine. The light is no longer an indicator of something wrong. Instead, it's just broken.

If anyone has a right to act out, it seems that a trauma victim would. Not all habits are unhealthy, but bad habits will cripple you and those around you. The US Department of Health and Human Services Substance Abuse and Mental Health Administration produced an anger management manual that states:

> Anger can become a routine, familiar, and predictable response to a variety of situations. When anger is displayed frequently and aggressively, it can become a maladaptive habit. A habit, by definition, means performing behaviors automatically, over and over again, without thinking. The frequent and aggressive expression of anger can be viewed as a maladaptive habit because it results in negative consequences.[4]

The manual, produced in 2002 and reprinted in 2008, goes on to state, "You can break the anger habit by becoming aware of the events and circumstances that trigger your anger and the negative consequences that result from it." In my own experience working with people who struggle managing their anger, I have heard countless stories about the consequences. From broken relationships and lost employment to hospitalizations and legal problems, the consequences of anger can be far reaching: having the FBI show up at your door, being accused of attempted murder, running someone off the road, having lifelong scars or injuries. It wasn't worth it to any of these individuals. Yes, these are extreme examples. But what about a friendship ending, turmoil in your family, embarrassment, or feeling bad about yourself? You must make a choice. Romans 12:2 tells us not to be conformed but to be transformed.

Has anger become a habit for you? If it has, how does it show up in your life? In what ways has your anger resulted in negative consequences? There is no real evidence that it takes (or *only* takes) twenty-one days to break a habit, but today is the best day to get started. You can break the cycle. Start your transformation now!

Do you know the story of Anna the Prophetess from Luke 2? Anna was a widow after only seven years of marriage, and she remained a widow for the rest of her life. But instead of allowing anger to become her habit, her way of life, she spent her life worshipping, fasting, and praying. Can you think of additional ways to break the anger habit?

4. Mask

Anger is often used as a mask to cover up a strong sense of guilt, embarrassment, or disgrace, which are common among people dealing with trauma or overwhelming life events. Some people transform these feelings into frustrations because, believe it or not, anger is the easier emotion to deal with. Anger may be more manageable than anxiety. Frustration may be easier to handle than helplessness. Irritation is not quite as difficult as depression. Friend, can you look at yourself, and your true emotions, openly and honestly? If not, you will likely replace difficult emotions with anger. Using anger as a mask for other emotions is a defense mechanism that prolongs the problems and allows you to blame others for how you feel and, unfortunately, postpone the healing process. Yes, managing anger is difficult. Taking off the anger mask and dealing with other emotions is difficult. But this is all very necessary in order to achieve and maintain emotional stability and deepen your relationship with Christ. If you're struggling with managing your anger, perhaps the following two questions will help you process your thoughts and prayers about how you can heal and grow in this area.

1. Read Romans 12:2. What does this mean to you and how can you apply it to anger management?

_____

_____

_____

_____

2. Instead of complaining or controlling, what does the Bible say about managing upsetting events and dealing with those who have wronged you? Find some Scripture references, and write the verses out in your journal. You can also write them on index cards and place them around your house and in your car to help you when you are tempted to become angry.

Women often wear these four faces of frustration—entitlement, habit, control, and mask—without even realizing it. We walk around believing our anger and frustration and irritation are warranted or justifiable. But what damage is being done as a result? Are we being harmed by the most egregious of these emotions, anger? In the following chapters, we'll answer that very question as we look at topics such as righteous versus unrighteous anger and myths of anger while also learning practical techniques to dissolve this whole anger thing.

CHAPTER 9

IS ANGER HURTING YOU?

"My dear brothers and sisters, take note of this:
Everyone should be quick to listen,
slow to speak and slow to become angry,
because human anger does not produce
the righteousness that God desires."

James 1:19–20

Now that we've explored some faces of frustration, we're going to look at
anger more in-depth. In this chapter you will learn more about righ-
teous versus unrighteous anger, and whether your anger is harmful. If
you realize that it is, you can start reining in what isn't helping you
find the hope and healing you desperately crave.

One sunny day after church, my husband was driving while we
were trying to decide what to eat for lunch. All of a sudden,
another car zoomed up behind us and pulled alongside our car

just before careening in front of us, barely missing the front end of our car. When we arrived at the next stoplight, that same driver slammed his car *in reverse* and started backing up as if he was going to ram into the front of our car. Fortunately, the light turned green and the car sped off. We can only assume we were not going fast enough for the driver of that car and he decided to teach us a lesson. What lesson did I learn? *Road rage is a problem!*

When we have experienced trauma, stress, or overwhelming life events, road rage is just one way that we might experience unrighteous anger.

Maybe you have been a passenger in a car with an angry driver. Maybe you were confronted with another motorist who acted like she was the only driver on the road. Maybe *you* were the angry driver.... I used to teach anger management classes, and I cannot begin to recount all the stories that involved angry drivers. I have worked with individuals who have experienced serious consequences as a result of their road rage. One was arrested and accused of attempted murder after a car followed him into a parking lot and he grabbed hold of a tire iron for self-defense. One landed in the hospital because of a serious knife wound. Another client had an illegal blaring horn installed in his car, and he honked it at someone he thought wasn't driving well. This loud blare startled the driver and forced her car off the road and into a telephone pole. The saddest story I ever heard, though, was told by a guy whose friend was left paraplegic as a result of his own road rage. All because of anger. How many of us are in similar conditions, or *could have been* in similar conditions, because of the lasting damage caused by our emotions running out of control?

You too may have a tendency to get mad while driving. You may have a tendency to be impatient with other drivers and consider your needs above everyone else's. You may tend to be competitive with other drivers and believe that you must win a self-created contest. You may believe it's your duty to teach other drivers a lesson for their perceived wrongdoings.[1] Unintentionally, you may be allowing your stress to come out in one or more of these ways while driving.

Perhaps you're perfectly calm on the road but other circumstances or people trigger you into feeling angry. If you easily become angry, whether you're driving or simply trying to have a conversation with someone, know that you're not alone. Everyone gets angry sometimes, and as we've already established, someone who's been through a traumatic event may get triggered more easily than someone who hasn't been traumatized. If that describes you, it's time to tackle your anger—before it wreaks any more havoc on your life.

OWN IT!

God knows the emotional toll that unrighteous anger can take on us as individuals, and He knows the impact it has on our relationships and on others around us. For example, anger is meant to indicate injustice, to empower, and to give boldness to use your voice and take action. But if the anger you experience as a result of frustrating triggers lasts longer than other emotions and leads to further negative consequences ("assault with deadly sarcasm" or abusive criticism, physical outrage, or the refusal to depend on God's justice), you most likely have a problem.

Attending to and managing explosive or overwhelming emotion is an ongoing challenge, seemingly impossible at first, but I assure you, it's not. By being aware of the source of your feelings, you can **make daily sane choices** that are vital to your life and to your loved ones. **Taking responsibility is the critical next step.** This means that instead of blaming others around you for your frustration, irritability, or anger, you have to *own* your emotions. It's not about what others have done or are doing to you, but what you are doing with your feelings. Taking responsibility means recognizing when your emotions influence you in such a way that not only alienates you from those you love, but also distances you from God.

Isn't it awesome to know that the God who created us *and* all of our emotions forgives us for the times we act in a way He did not intend as a result of those emotions? And He cleanses us of our wrongdoing and gives us chance after chance to do better the next time. Jesus "is faithful and just and will forgive us our sins and purify us from all unrighteousness" (1 John 1:9). When we fall down again, He forgives us again. Even the righteous [wo]man falls seven times, but she gets up again (Proverbs 24:16). Oh, how that sets my heart at ease! I hope the same is true for you. Even though I know God forgives us and gives us another chance, I don't want to hurt others, or God, by flying apart. You too? Let's ask the Lord to guide and direct us as we work to release our frustrations to Him.

This is *not* about obliterating frustration, irritation, or anger. That is impossible and impractical. (You can now release the breath you've been holding!) What are some realistic goals? Let's make three: (1) decrease the intensity, frequency, and negative consequences of overwhelming emotions; (2) develop a deeper relationship with Christ, whose amazing promise is that you can do all things through *Him* who gives you strength (Philippians 4:13); and (3) remember that the strength to master these often overwhelming emotions comes from the very One who created them. When you temper and befriend your emotions, even the dark ones, you will grow closer to God, have less conflict with others, experience fewer upsetting emotional and physical symptoms, and feel better about yourself.

GODLY VERSUS UNGODLY ANGER

Anger is demonstrated all throughout the Bible. For example, the religious leaders got angry with Jesus on more than one occasion: for His deeds (such as healing on the Sabbath), for His claims (such as the ability to forgive sins), and for His refusal to follow all of the religious laws. Jesus got angry too, but His anger was always righteous. For example, in John 2:13–16, Jesus found moneychangers in the temple. His *zeal* for His Father's house led to His anger (verse 17). In other words, Jesus became angry out of the great love He had for the Father and He would not tolerate the injustice of His Father's house being used for any unrighteous purpose. (God the Father got angry too—many times in the Old Testament. To learn more, read the verses listed near the end of this chapter.)

Okay, so you may *occasionally* get upset for the right reasons. But more often than not, you get angry over pretty insignificant issues. Right? (I do too, as indicated by the Spanx debacle!) *The resulting feelings and behaviors are what we're targeting here.* **Even if your anger is righteous, you need to ask yourself if your reactions are.** Say you become angry after witnessing a significant injustice, such as someone picking on a disabled person. This is righteous anger; however, if you take justice into your own hands through slugging the bully, your behavior is not righteous.

Our focus is centered on the onslaught of negative emotions and your resulting negative behaviors. We'll talk more about this later, but often it's aggressive behavior, rather than angry feelings, that causes us problems. By addressing both, you may find yourself developing the ability to release long-held anger and overcome the anger you experience about more serious issues as well. This is why addressing anger when talking about trauma, stress, and overwhelming life events is so important.

If you are sick and tired of letting anger dictate your life, then use this section of the book to help you work toward your goal of reducing the intensity and frequency of your anger and grow closer to Jesus in the process. As a reference point, it may be helpful to identify how prone you are to anger and whether you have difficulty in managing your anger. Complete the following questionnaire to get a better grasp of your current anger management concerns. (Note: I am using *angry*, *frustrated*, and *irritated* as synonyms, although some may argue they are on a spectrum where anger is the most extreme and irritated is the least extreme.)

IS YOUR ANGER HURTING YOU?

(Respond to each statement by writing either "true" or "false" in the blank.)[2]

Part A: "Am I prone to anger?"

1. I feel tense a lot of the time. _____
2. People often tell me I need to calm down. _____
3. I get angry very quickly. _____
4. I stay angry for a long time. _____
5. It seems like everything makes me angry. _____
6. Minor troubles annoy me. _____
7. I often blame my troubles on other people. _____
8. When I feel wronged, I want revenge. _____
9. Anger makes me feel powerful and in control. _____
10. I am still angry about bad things from my past. _____
11. I get into a lot of arguments. _____
12. I get very upset when things don't go my way. _____

Part B: "How do I handle anger?"

1. I store up anger until I'm about to explode. _____
2. I try to ignore my anger in the hope it will go away. _____
3. When angry, I say or do things that I later regret. _____

4. My anger frightens me. _____

5. My anger frightens others. _____

6. When I get angry, I:

    a. yell or scream _____

    b. cry _____

    c. break things _____

    d. hurt myself _____

    e. hurt others _____

7. My anger has resulted in problems at work or home. _____

8. My anger has resulted in problems with the law. _____

9. I use alcohol or other drugs to help mask my anger. _____

10. I have tried to control my anger and failed. _____

11. I feel out of control when I get angry. _____

12. I want help managing my anger. _____

If you wrote "true" in any blank next to the twelve questions in part A, you are likely *prone to anger*. If you wrote "true" in any blank next to the twelve questions in part B, you likely have *difficulty managing* your anger. In the next chapter, we'll take a deeper look at why it's so important to address this aspect of emotion, especially for those who have PTSD or are still affected by a tough life experience. But first, I've included some Bible verses and questions for you to consider as you think through your own anger and compare it to righteous anger.

1. Read James 1:19–20. What do these verses mean to you? How might you apply them to your life?

_____

_____

_____

_____

_____

2. Read the following Scripture verses:

      a. Exodus 4:14

      b. Exodus 22:22–24

      c. Exodus 32:10

      d. Deuteronomy 6:14–15

      e. Judges 2:13–14

      f. Ezra 8:22

      g. Mark 3:5

      h. John 2:13–22

All of the Old Testament verses listed reference the anger of God, while the New Testament verses reference the anger of Jesus Christ. What did you learn about the anger of God and Jesus by reading through these verses?

_____

_____

_____

_____

_____

3. Think of a time when *you* experienced righteous anger. Now think of a time when your frustrated feelings were uncalled for. Describe the difference in the consequences (i.e., what you thought about yourself, how you felt about yourself, etc.).

_____

_____

_____

_____

_____

Now that we've looked at some of the differences between righteous anger and unrighteous anger, let's nail down some of the excuses that block us from seeing the truth—justifications we claim but that usually point to the fact that our anger is not warranted.

CHAPTER 10

NO MORE EXCUSES: MYTH BUSTING

"Therefore, if anyone is in Christ, the new creation has come:
The old has gone, the new is here!"

2 Corinthians 5:17

There are many excuses that women tell themselves in order to ratio-
nalize anger. It's tough to consider, but often we make these excuses
so that we don't have to take responsibility for our emotions or, more
importantly, their consequences. Five excuses, and the truths to counter
them, are explored in this chapter—including hormones! It's time to
stop making excuses and start taking control by putting mind over
matter. Reclaiming your best self means replacing aggressiveness with
assertiveness, as seen in the powerful story of Queen Esther.

You know the classic story where the wife is constantly upset with
her husband: He leaves his laundry all over the house, the deck still
hasn't been stained, and he isn't very attentive to the kids. He's a

wonderful provider but seems to work all the time. She tries to be patient, but once she's *had enough*, she goes off like a ticking time bomb. Totally oblivious to the impact his choices have on her, he tells her she's acting "crazy," to which she retorts, "You made me this way!"

The story takes on many different forms, but the plot is the same: it's the story of women who blame others for their anger, buying into the lie that they can't help it if other people make them mad. It's just one myth we're going to bust in this chapter.

Exodus 34:6 tells us that God is slow to anger. I'm sure we'd all like to be more like that, but we simply can't be slow to anger if we use excuses in order to rationalize our anger and not take responsibility for it. (Ouch, right?) While there are many myths women believe and use to excuse anger, let's identify, explore, and then bust up five myths that hijack happiness and then apply the truths that reveal the lie of each one.

Myth #1: "If I don't get angry, people will think I'm weak."
Truth #1: The Lord's strength is perfected in our weakness (2 Corinthians 12:9). Will you allow God to take the limitations and weaknesses you currently experience and turn them into strengths? By taking itty-bitty baby steps toward choosing your emotions, you allow God's supernatural strength to do its work. It is much more difficult to stay calm than it is to lose control. If you first ask for God's strength in keeping your emotions level, others will begin to see you as a person of strength instead of a person who can't manage your emotions and behaviors. This

leads to an opportunity to share with others where the change they see in you comes from. Not only will you and your loved ones benefit, but this new approach to living can also be a powerful witnessing tool.

Myth #2: "I shouldn't keep my anger bottled up."
Truth #2: We don't have to keep anger bottled up or allow it to explode. You don't have to keep these emotions buried inside. However, you also don't have to let them out in an aggressive manner. According to the Substance Abuse and Mental Health Services Administration (SAMHSA), "Venting anger in an aggressive manner reinforces aggressive behavior."[1] Instead, you can and should learn how to manage frustration and irritability. This may mean anticipating scenarios and discerning when to speak and when to remain still or learning how to respond assertively rather than reacting aggressively during times of tension. This means that you are able to wisely distinguish between issues that need to be addressed and those that don't. See the upcoming discussion for more about assertiveness versus aggressiveness. For now, keep in mind that managing anger is not the same as keeping it bottled up inside. We can take a mindful approach to our lives and choose not to allow tempers to flare every time life doesn't go as smoothly as we'd like.

Myth #3: "Anger is healthy."
Truth #3: Anger can cause health problems, but it won't resolve them. The *desire* to be listened to, taken seriously, and

to be seen are all normal expectations in relationships and are actually quite healthy. The *demand* for these responses, however, is not. When people become frequently, intensely irate, they may experience bothersome and, with enough time, danger-ous physical and emotional symptoms. Is high blood pressure healthy? Teeth grinding? Gastric distress such as acid stomach, nausea, or diarrhea? Shortness of breath? Is a high level of anx-iety healthy? No! However, many people experience these and other symptoms while angry. The truth is, anger is *not* healthy. What feels like a release after "blowing up" is often a growing addiction to the high level of adrenaline that kicks in. If the source of the anger is not resolved, the scenario will play out again. The problem is that after abusing adrenaline over and over, it's like revving up a car engine and leaving it there to idle for too long; eventually the effects of anger damage the heart and arteries. We'll talk more about how to relieve daily stress later on in the book.

Myth #4: "I can't help it if others make me angry."
Truth #4: Your emotional responses are your responsibility.
For many people, this is the most difficult myth to face. It can be very easy to blame others for our frustrations. For example, how many times have you said, "You make me so mad," or, "She (or he) makes me so mad," or, "That makes me so angry"? Those simple statements take away our own responsibility and place it on others. It's easy to do when we have been wronged. When people hurt us, we can acknowledge their harmful behaviors. But

how can we blame others for our emotions? No one is forcing us to be angry. Of course, there are triggers for our irritability or anger, like the baby crying while the cell phone rings and when the latest Crock-Pot recipe doesn't turn out "Pinterest perfect," but we have to accept that our emotions are our own.

Only you can control yourself. Try changing the way you think and speak about this. Instead of saying, "My husband *made me* mad," try saying, "*I got angry* at my husband." Through this simple change, you are taking ownership of your anger instead of blaming someone else. This is truly a challenge, but the outcome is well worth it.

Myth #5: "Don't blame me—it's my hormones!"
Truth #5: Remedies abound for managing moods during "that time of the month." God made women unique and wonderful, and this includes the way our hormones work and control our reproductive systems. While irritability can certainly come packaged with premenstrual syndrome (PMS), it should not be used as an excuse to act in an aggressive manner. If you are one who tends to have trouble during this time, there are ways to manage your moods. For example, exercise, get a massage, do some other relaxing activity, or spend time with a friend. Use a mindful approach of repeating the truth to yourself that this is only a short-lived time of your month and that it will soon pass. (See chapter 16 for more on using a mindful approach.) Essentially, take care of yourself instead of allowing the frustrations to build up.

Note: If you have severe symptoms, you may be experiencing pre-menstrual dysphoric disorder. This is a serious disorder that should be evaluated and treated by qualified professionals. Please share your symptoms with your health-care provider for appropriate treatment.

Now that we've debunked some myths, let's go over some practical ways you can help yourself manage anger.

START AN ANGER JOURNAL

Start keeping track of episodes during which you are frustrated, irritable, or angry. You can do this by using the example of a journal provided below. You can also use the forms provided in appendix B. Following each episode, note the date and time of your experience, the activator for your emotions, the level of emotion using a scale of 1 to 10 (with 1 being very minimal and 10 being very extreme), your response to the emotions, and how you felt after the emotions subsided. This may seem like a big assignment, but it will give you great information.

At the end of the week, review your journal and look for patterns. For example, do you frequently get upset with the same person(s)? Do you frequently feel guilty after an episode? Do you find that you are most likely to get upset right after getting home from work? Patterns can reveal a lot of important information that can help you discern what action to take to better manage negative emotions. Keeping track of these episodes will help you identify those patterns.

DATE AND TIME	ACTIVATOR	WARNING SIGNS	RATING (1-10)	REACTION	HOW I FELT LATER

As you work on managing your own anger, it is wise to recognize the warning signs of others in your life getting angry. As you know from personal experience, you can't reason with someone who is in the midst of an anger episode. If you find yourself in a situation in which someone may become aggressive with you, get to a safe place. **And if you are experiencing violence at the hands of someone in your home, please call the domestic violence hotline at 1-800-799-SAFE.**

I love the New Living Translation version of Romans 8:38. It says, "And I am convinced that nothing can ever separate us from God's love. Neither death nor life, neither angels nor demons, *neither our fears for today nor our worries about tomorrow*—not even the powers of hell can separate us from God's love." Don't you love the line I've italicized? Our fears won't separate us from God's love. Our worries about tomorrow won't either.

BE ASSERTIVE, *NOT* AGGRESSIVE

"He guides the humble in what is right and teaches them his way."
Psalm 25:9

It's the *act* of aggression that gets most people into trouble, *not* their anger. As we've already established, anger can lead to aggression, which can be dangerous and have serious consequences. It is important to understand the difference between aggressiveness and assertiveness, because in most situations, the appropriate response is assertiveness, which is a way of demonstrating respect while also standing up for your own rights. The goal of being assertive is to *influence* instead of *force*. Remember the old saying "It's not what you say; it's how you say it"? Instead of blaming others, accept responsibility for your emotions, and you will decrease the chances that the person you are angry with will respond defensively and increase the likelihood that they will hear your request to change their behavior. In being assertive, you increase the chance of a behavior change and you decrease defensiveness!

One method of being assertive involves the following four steps, widely encouraged by mental health providers, which you can use when you become upset with someone:

1. Describe the problem situation to the person.
2. Tell the person how you choose to feel about his or her behavior.
3. Tell the person how his or her behavior affects you.
4. Suggest a new behavior that you would prefer.

This matters. You matter. Your sanity matters. You can, and should, have a firm and confident stance when delivering your assertive message. Squarely look the other person in the eye and use a confident tone of voice. If the other person becomes angry or tearful, that is *his or her* decision. However, keep in mind that just because we ask for something assertively doesn't mean we'll get it. The goal here is to move from anger and aggression to irritation and assertiveness.

Even if you don't get what you want by being assertive, you can still avoid the guilt and shame you would have felt had you acted aggressively. Practice being assertive by following the steps below.

Assertiveness Practice

Complete the following using a situation you recently experienced:

Step 1: When you _____

Step 2: I chose to feel _____

Step 3: Because your behavior _____

Step 4: In the future I would prefer that you _____

ESTHER'S STORY

Esther is a famed biblical heroine in the Old Testament and a perfect example of effective assertiveness. The book of Esther tells her harrowing story after being chosen to be the Queen of Persia. An official of the king was offended when a Jewish man (who happened to be Esther's guardian, Mordecai) did not bow to him, so he petitioned the king to have all the Jews killed. Mordecai learned of this plot and begged Esther to use her position and favor with the king to attempt to save her people. Esther must have known that being aggressive would have resulted in grave consequences, but she also had no guarantee that being *assertive* would result in positive consequences, because even she was not allowed to go to the king without being summoned. Despite her fear, she was assertive during a crisis.

Esther knew the issue had to be addressed, and she was willing to trust in God. So she bravely walked (no doubt trembling every step along the way) to see the king and plead for her people. The king sided with Esther and had his own official, rather than the Jewish people, killed.

Esther was afraid and worried, but she knew she had God on her side. She knew He loved her and would be with her as she approached the king. Esther 4:14 sets the scene for the famous words that Mordecai asked Esther, "And who knows but that you have come to your royal position for such a time as this?" Regardless of what has happened to us in the past, we can trust God and His Word instead of the myths we tell ourselves and the lies Satan spews.

Put on Your Armor

You have learned about excuses we tell ourselves and the truths to counter them. But what should we do about those lies from our enemy, Satan? According to John 8:44, Satan is the "Father of Lies." It's not only what he does, but it's who he is. He uses lies to mess with our thoughts and feelings. But there is a way to counter his lies. Take a moment to read Ephesians 6:10–18, a description of the armor of God. How might each piece of the armor of God help protect you against Satan's lure to become aggressive when angry?

Belt of truth: _____

Breastplate of righteousness: _____

Ready feet: _____

Shield of faith: _____

Helmet of salvation: _____

Sword of the Spirit: _____

Your armor will help protect you from the enemy, and it can help you better manage your thoughts and feelings. There are also other helpful techniques that can be used to conquer intense emotions. We'll look at a couple of methods in the next chapter.

CHAPTER 11

CONQUERING INTENSE EMOTIONS

"What is impossible with man is possible with God."
Luke 18:27

This chapter focuses on a proven therapeutic method of evaluating beliefs that lead to anger and changing the beliefs that are not helpful. It uses a technique pulled from cognitive behavioral therapy: "A" is for activator, "B" is for belief, "C" is for consequence, "D" is for disputing bad beliefs, "E" is for effective belief, "F" is for new feeling. After gaining clarity about the whos and whys of your anger, you then can begin developing what I call an Anger Authority Plan.

You may be wondering why we're still discussing anger in this book. You may be thinking you got enough from the previous chapters on anger and don't need to learn anything more. You might even be thinking you're not angry at all. But I want to make sure we cover anger thoroughly because most people who are dealing with trauma, stressful situations, or overwhelming circumstances feel angry at some point. And like a cancer left untreated, anger can spread and cause untold problems. The tools in this chapter will help you reduce—or possibly eliminate—the effects anger has on your life and your relationships.

Do you ever want to hide your head under the covers, burrow down to the foot of the bed, rather than have to deal with others—and conflict? Been there! Let me encourage you in this: instead of avoiding people, we can and must change our angry responses. Did you know these responses begin in your heart and then come out in your words and actions? Did you also know that it is *not* life's circumstances that make you angry but rather how you choose to think about those circumstances? Remember the words of Elizabeth Kenny (an Australian nun), "He who angers you, conquers you!"

You do have power and control over your emotions, and I'll show you how with a simple path to follow with the ABCs of anger.[1] In this chapter, you will learn how to identify what triggers anger, what beliefs lead to anger, and what consequences you experience as a result of your anger. But it doesn't stop there! You can then learn how to dispute the anger-producing beliefs, replace them with more helpful beliefs, and experience a reduction in negative consequences, including the anger itself!

ABCS OF ANGER

Activators. An activator is something or someone that triggers your anger. You have 0 percent control over the activators in your life. For example, your husband's snoring, the dog barking, the slowpoke driver in front of you when you are already late for work. List some of your own activators here.

_____

_____

_____

Beliefs. These are what you *think* about the activators. In other words, what you tell yourself about the activators. You have 100 percent control over your beliefs about a particular activator. For example, you think the slowpoke driver should get out of *your* way. That is your belief. This thought leads to your consequences. What do you tell yourself about the activators you encounter?

_____

_____

_____

Consequences. These are the emotions you experience, the behaviors you engage in, and the physical responses you create for yourself when you hold certain beliefs about the activators. Here are some examples of the various consequences:

1. Emotions: anger, irritation, frustration, cynicism

2. Behaviors: hitting, cursing, throwing things, yelling, stomping, slamming doors

3. Physical: heart racing, increased blood pressure, shaky hands, stomach upset

With the slowpoke driver example, you may start to feel irritated. Maybe you are saying (loudly), "Come on! Get out of the way!" As the volume of your voice increases, your heart starts to race. These consequences are happening so quickly that you believe you don't have time to think and avoid them. What negative consequences have you experienced? Write about some consequences you've experienced for some of the activators and beliefs you mentioned above. Let them motivate you to slow down and work on taking control of your emotions.

_____

_____

_____

Disputing. This is a means of dismantling anger-producing beliefs and finding a new way of thinking. Just because beliefs are in our minds doesn't make them true. (Isn't that a revelation!) Just because you believe that slowpoke driver should get out of your way does not mean you are right.

Here is where you challenge those thoughts. For example, you can ask yourself questions such as, "Where is it written that I own this road and everyone should get out of my way when I'm driving?

Just because I am running late, what makes me think I have the right to speed? Who made me queen of the road?" Funny, I know, but so true! And, sister, you really can go through this entire ABC process for even your most serious activators and beliefs. In fact, these ABCs are one of the most common interventions used in psychotherapy. Now, try disputing the beliefs you listed above:

_____

_____

_____

Effective beliefs. This is where you replace your anger-producing beliefs with effective beliefs. You still may experience frustration or irritation, but you have a better chance of addressing and managing them when you are honest with yourself. How about thinking, *I need to leave for work earlier so I don't get stuck in traffic and become frustrated.* After coming up with this replacement, this effective belief, you can make plans to change your behaviors so they match your new beliefs. Do you have any other ideas?

_____

_____

_____

Feelings. When you substitute effective beliefs for anger-producing beliefs, you will not experience anywhere near the same level of consequences as you would otherwise. Once you have a new thought, you can have a new feeling. Yep, a reduction in the anger you are so sick of experiencing. Can you think of any possible new feelings you'd like to experience instead of the anger, frustration, or irritation?

_____

_____

_____

Are you holding on to harmful emotions? Can you dispute your original beliefs, come up with more effective beliefs, and develop new feelings? It's much better than holding on to that old anger. Remember, you can do all things through Christ who gives you strength (Philippians 4:13). Try going through the A–F steps with your own example:

Activator: List your activator and describe the situation in which you felt angry.

_____

_____

Belief: What is your belief or thought about this situation?

_____

_____

Consequence: Describe what happened for you as a result of this situation.

    Emotional: _____

    Behavioral: _____

    Physical: _____

Disputing: Take some time to challenge your original thought. Think, *Where is it written that* ... Jot down some thoughts below.

_____

_____

Effective belief: Now that you have disputed your original belief, what is your new thought about this situation?

_____

_____

Feelings *(new!)*: How do you feel now? Have your physical and behavioral consequences changed as well? List your new emotions here.

_____

_____

The ABCs are an effective introductory exercise to bring clarity about where your anger starts, the path it usually takes, and how you can change beliefs to redirect it. The ABCs will set you up to then take the next steps in creating a proactive plan. Your own tailor-made Anger Authority Plan is another practical therapeutic tool you can put to use without seeing a mental health professional. Before we go there, let me share a story with you. When I first met Jan, I was speaking with a group of women about how people can become so stressed or overwhelmed that their tempers flare.

JAN'S STORY

One of the attendees of a session I was leading tentatively raised her hand to share her recent experience. Jan was still grieving the loss of a parent. As a result, she felt more sensitive than usual. Much like when we are already sick and our immune system is suppressed, making us more susceptible to further illness, Jan's ability to tolerate stress was decreased because of her weakened emotional state.

One day Jan was looking for a ruler in a desk drawer. While the item she was looking for wasn't in the drawer, the drawer got stuck and would not slide back into the desk. No matter how hard she tried, Jan could not get that drawer back in. All she needed was the tap of a hammer, she thought, to get the drawer past its sticking place.

Still no success. As her frustration turned to raging anger, she decided she *was* going to get that drawer back in. Using the hammer, she gave it a sturdier hit. Instead of sliding into place, the drawer began to fall apart. Something snapped within Jan. Without stopping, she beat on that old desk drawer, taking out all her pent-up emotions, until it was nothing but firewood kindling.

Clearly, Jan was not just angry about the desk drawer. Her out-of-control anger was merely the mask for significant emotional pain and, being at a loss for how to cope with her grief, reduced her ability to tolerate frustration.

Jan knew she needed help. She worked through the ABCs to establish where she'd been emotionally and why she'd smashed the drawer to smithereens. She certainly did not want a repeat performance. As Jan works to manage the pieces of her current problem puzzle, the ABCs will be an important aspect of her recovery.

If the anger is connected to a personal relationship, the relationship continues to suffer. Often, this anger becomes displaced. In other words, anger starts being expressed toward yourself or others or even inanimate objects instead of toward the activator. People do this for one of several reasons. For example, the activator may be too powerful or too negative. It could be that your anger is really toward a business or institution, making it very difficult to resolve (except within yourself). Perhaps the activator is no longer in your life and is not accessible, or it may even be deceased. Regardless of where the anger is coming from or to whom (or what) it is directed, you can learn to manage your anger by developing a plan. It's easy to believe that you will "cross that bridge when you get to it," but the problem is that if you come up to a bridge and you aren't ready to cross it, you either turn right around, get stuck where you are, or blow it up. The Anger Authority Plan will help you forge ahead.

DEVELOPING YOUR ANGER AUTHORITY PLAN

Follow the steps below to successfully develop your own Anger Authority Plan.

1. *Set attainable goals.* Your goals should be reasonable. Try setting short-term *and* long-term goals, but don't set too many

goals at once. You want to be able to accomplish your goals. For example, if you find yourself hitting a 10 on a 1-to-10 anger scale (where 10 is "through the roof" mad) a few times a week, a short-term goal may be to reduce this anger to no higher than an 8 within a couple of weeks and a long-term goal may be to reduce this anger to no higher than a 5 within a couple of months.

2. *Determine your action plan.* In other words, how are you going to go about trying to accomplish your goals? Be as specific as you can here, but know that there will be many more techniques provided throughout the remainder of this book that you can add to your action list if they work for you.

3. *Set a time frame for when you want to accomplish a goal.* Make sure your time frame is reasonable. For example, if your anger reaches an 8 four times a week, it is highly unlikely that it will decrease to a 4 two times a week within a week's time. That is a better long-term goal. For now, maybe try not going over a 6 three times a week. This is a good short-term goal.

4. *Reward yourself!* You are never too old to benefit from positive reinforcement. When you reach a goal, reward yourself with something positive. But please, make sure it's something within reason. I once failed to mention that part to a client and the client reported the reward was eating an entire large pizza at one sitting. Don't do that!

5. *Get support from family and friends.* Who can you call when you need a compassionate, listening ear or someone to help calm you down so you can continue making progress on your management plan? I encourage you to talk with a spouse, mentor, pastor,

and/or trusted friend to get the accountability you need. If you need more assistance than your loved one can provide, you can (and should!) seek help from a mental health professional.

Now it's time to develop your own plan to claim authority over your anger. Use this chart to track your progress.

"MY ANGER AUTHORITY PLAN"

GOAL	ACTION PLAN	TARGET DATE	REWARD?

As you notice the progress you're making on anger authority, here are a couple of questions to consider:

1. Proverbs is a book about godly living. Read Proverbs 3:5–6 and 21:5. What do these verses say to you about planning?

_____

_____

_____

_____

2. In the space provided, write out the names of people you can ask to pray for and support you while working toward your anger authority goals.

_____

_____

_____

_____

Jan was relieved to know that she was not alone in experiencing anger after a traumatic event and that there is hope and healing for her and those in similar situations. The same can be true for you. As you work on these exercises both now and in the future, remember that the Lord directs the steps of the godly (Psalm 37:23). This is future oriented! Instead of being stuck at a bridge you're too afraid to cross, you will be prepared to move forward. You do not have to be a prisoner of your past. If you'd like to explore anger management more in-depth, a free anger management manual can be found at http://store.samhsa.gov/shin/content//SMA13-4213/SMA13-4213.pdf.

CHAPTER 12

KNOWING WHO YOU REALLY ARE

*"For you created my inmost being; you knit
me together in my mother's womb."*

Psalm 139:13

*As the writers of the Psalms struggle to find resolve, they ultimately end
in the voices of praise to the great God of the nation Israel—the same
God we worship today. When we turn to God in our daily victories
and sufferings, we find that God is the giver of our identity. The Psalms
act as our declaration, reminding us again and again about what gives
us our purpose, and reminding us of whose we are.*

The night before my high school graduation, my younger sister and
I lay in the dark bedroom we shared. Having difficulty getting to
sleep, I stared at the shadows on the ceiling. After a few moments,
I finally whispered a fear I had to my sister. It wasn't about going

to college or being on my own. No, nothing really that important at all. Instead it was this:

"What if I don't graduate with honors?"

We had not yet received our final grades, and I didn't know if I would have the GPA to graduate with honors. I actually never liked the *learning* part of school. I took honors courses but often did just enough to get by. I read too many CliffsNotes and not enough books. I couldn't tell you the difference between types of triangles. (And I don't mind saying that I have never used any geometry formulas. Ever. In my whole life. Except on those awful high school tests. Thank God for a great tutor.) But I did care about doing well in school, and I wanted to graduate with honors.

My "baby" sister, four years younger than me but frequently my encourager, reminded me in her sweet way that even if I didn't get a gold cord draped over my shoulders, *it was okay*. I was still going to be a high school graduate (!) and still going to college (!). Her words echoed in my mind as I drifted off to sleep.

The next morning when I arrived at the auditorium where all the local high school graduations took place, I grabbed my graduation book as soon we sat down in our chairs to search for the double-asterisk indicator that I was in fact graduating with honors. Breathing a sigh of relief (which I literally did again as I typed those words—right here in the middle of Panera), I sat down with a smile on my face. That is until the girl in front of me whipped around to exclaim: "*You're* graduating with honors?" Out of the blue. Just like that. With a mix of defeat and defiance, I looked squarely into her stunned face and shot back, "*Yes*, I am."

With her mouth agape, she snapped her head back around to face the front, and I sat there with pride—and a knot of hurt in the middle of my stomach.

I celebrated hard that day with family and friends. And by *hard*, I mean we ate Lots. Of. Cake. It wasn't long before I was loading up my mama's station wagon to head to college, wearing my favorite yellow tank top. And while the days were long, the years were short, and before I knew it, I was graduating. With my bachelor's degree. Then with my master's. And then with a doctor of philosophy. Each time I was taunted with a niggling self-doubt and insecurity that I was not smart enough to walk across that stage, I promised myself I would continue to work harder than I had ever worked before—and never to let anyone's opinion about me influence who I was or what I was going to do. Instead, I was going to do what God called me to do.

I want the same for you. After a good number of years of bumps, scrapes, false starts, and restarts, I finally *know within the fibers of my being* that we are not merely defined by the fabric of the family we originated from, nor are we the product of who someone else says or thinks we are. Our value is not even determined by man-made awards and recognition such as degrees or honor cords. Somewhere in our DNA we know this, but we still struggle to believe that *we are who God says we are.*

WORDS THAT WOUND

Words spoken by others matter to us, and the focus here is on their impact. Perhaps you've experienced the damaging effects of mean girls or online bullying. Regardless of how or when they arrive, when people are ugly to us, it hurts. A loved one of mine who was physically and emotionally abused as a child once told me that the bruising blows of verbal abuse she received were worse than the physical abuse. She said the physical wounds healed, but the hurtful words scarred and have stayed with her for decades. The words that others speak over us tend to be the loudest voices playing in our heads, drowning out even the words of Jesus.

Sometimes it's not the exact words but the deeper meaning that cripples and makes us limp. For me, the question asked that graduation day in June many years ago was really a haunting statement: "You're not smart." Even though I didn't love academics at the time, the words still stung. Although I knew my parents would be proud of me regardless of my lot in life, I wanted to make them proud—and prove I could keep up with my four brilliant siblings. Even to this day, this fear of others thinking I'm stupid is triggered by unsuspecting people.

When I perceive that a person is being patronizing, talking down to me, or treating me as if I'm not on their level, I become overly defensive. In my mind (and sometimes out loud) I say, *I am not stupid. Stop treating me as if I am!* Though the tape in my head seems to have an automatic play button, one which I can choose to turn off, I often take on the label that I believe someone else is placing on me—regardless if they actually are. But the truth is I don't have to accept that broken belief. You don't have to either.

WHO DEFINES US

We are *not* defined by who others think or say we are. We are not even who we have worked so hard to be or believe we are. Honors, corporate ladders, and titles are all man-made distinctions—and distractions. God is not more pleased with gold tassels than with those who care for the poor or feed the hungry. In Matthew 20, Jesus told the parable of the workers in the vineyard. He described the kingdom of heaven as being like a landowner who went out to hire workers for his vineyard. Although the workers were hired at different times throughout the day, they were all paid the same. Why? Because they each had agreed to work for that amount. The landowner was completely fair to each person, challenging the grumbling workers by asking them if they were envious that he was being generous.

Jesus stated in verse 16, "So the last will be first, and the first will be last." We American Christians have trouble accepting this as the standard for us too. Surely this can't be right. We can't possibly all receive the same grace from God, can we? Doesn't it matter who we are in this world? Don't we have to be *somebody*? The truth is that we are who God says we are, and God says a lot about us. Look at a few verses from the book of Ephesians:

Ephesians 1:4 says God chose us.

Ephesians 1:7 tells us we are forgiven.

Ephesians 2:10 states we are *His* workmanship (not our own).

Let's not stop here. We learn in 1 Corinthians 6:19 that we are God's temple, in John 1:12 that we are God's children, and in

John 15:15 that we are friends of Jesus. Oh, sisters, the Bible tells us a lot about who we are as believers in Christ. We cannot allow the world or even well-meaning friends and family to wrongly define and label us. When you start to hear that lying voice in your head saying you are not good enough, pretty enough, rich enough, or that you are not smart enough, that you deserved that horrible thing that happened to you, *stop* right there and tell yourself (yell it out loud if you have to):

"No, I am not stupid. I am God's workmanship!"

"No, I am not unloved or unwanted. I am a friend of Jesus!"

"No, I do not deserve to be abused. I am a temple of God!"

Sometimes the lying voice you hear is your own, and Christ wants to be heard above it. My aunt Lib reminded me of this years ago. When I was in the throes of my doctoral program, Aunt Lib, in the midst of the evermore laborious journey of cancer treatment, called to tell me how proud she was of me. But instead of talking so much about her pride in my educational accomplishments, she shared how she was most proud of me for accepting Jesus Christ as Savior and Lord and for seeking to follow Him. You see, accomplishments (while they should be celebrated) are not what make us good enough. What makes us enough is that we are transformed by the mercies of Christ Jesus—as Lou knows firsthand.

LOU'S STORY

Lou believed she was fat. Regardless of the fact that she remained well below a healthy weight, she could not be convinced otherwise. In her mind, she could never be skinny enough. As a result, she ate scarce amounts, and when she did eat, she would force herself to vomit. Treatment, including medical and psychiatric hospitalizations, would help for a while, but Lou always returned to power and control over her life through not eating, the relentless felt need for many people who struggle with eating disorders.

Lou was looking to control *something* in her life after experiencing two different traumatic events. First, she had been sexually assaulted; and second, her young son had died. Initially, Lou turned to food to comfort herself. She gained an excessive amount of weight, and when she could no longer deny that she'd become morbidly obese, she decided to do something about it. Unfortunately, she went from one extreme to the other, from eating too much to eating too little. She could only see herself as a fat woman who needed to lose weight. This is the message Lou told herself over and over. Because she could not change her past, and she could not seem to control her emotions over the past, she exerted power over food.

Lou needed the power of God's truth. With professional help and guidance, she is now reminding herself daily—sometimes hourly—of these truths, with what we refer to as "renewing the mind," bathing our wayward thoughts with the truth of who God is and who He says we are. While this is a difficult path to walk, it is so much better than the alternative—turning away from our creator and redeemer and choosing to rely on old methods that have failed over and over again.

GLORIOUS BRIDE

When Christ looks on us, His bride (the church, His followers), He sees His glory. What does it mean to see ourselves as He sees us? On my wedding day when the doors opened and everyone turned to stand and look at me, I burst into tears. My mother shared with me later that instead of looking at the bride, she looks at the groom. She wants to see the bride through the groom's eyes by watching his expression upon first seeing his beloved looking so beautiful when she appears and begins walking toward him. On my wedding day, my mother looked at my soon-to-be husband and knew without a doubt how much he loved me.

Can we even dare to imagine the look on the face of our Savior when we, His bride, meet Him face to face? And how will we react? I think of the song by Mercy Me, "I Can Only Imagine."*

> Surrounded by your glory
> What will my heart feel?
> Will I dance for you Jesus,
> Or in awe of you be still?
> Will I stand in your presence,
> Or to my knees will I fall?
> Will I sing Hallelujah,
> Will I be able to speak at all?
> I can only imagine.

How will Jesus react to seeing His precious ones for whom He died? Seeing *you*. Some people don't like to read the last book of the Bible, Revelation. They find it difficult to understand and somewhat scary. But I love it. It is a reminder of how much the triune God loves us.

In chapter 3, I wrote about the fall of man. The story took place in the first book of the Bible in which Satan successfully tempted Eve and Adam to sin. If we fast-forward to the last book of the Bible, Revelation, we see Satan's attempts to draw in the world to him and how many fall for his deceptive ways. Yet God continues to give people chance after chance to come to Him because of His love. I don't know how Jesus will react when He sees me, and I can only imagine what it will be like when our eyes first meet, but I'm sure it will be a beautiful and everlasting marriage. Sister, it's the same for all who believe in Jesus as Savior. We are called His!

In Isaiah 61:3, God reveals that His desire is to bestow on you a crown of beauty instead of ashes. We've all seen beauty from ashes. The only explanation for this is that God loves us. He does not cause bad things to happen to us, but we live in a fallen world where sin happens. And it's not just our own sin that causes us conflict. As most any woman reading this book can attest, the sin of others can certainly cause incredible pain. Lou can relate to that. Her trauma led to not only significant emotional pain but also the very harmful behaviors and effects of an eating disorder. Her mental health problems are significant enough that she will likely need some treatment for the rest of her life, but she has come a long way in her healing—emotionally, physically, and spiritually.

Lou continues to work toward speaking the truth about who she is to herself instead of allowing the hateful, lying voice that developed after her traumatic events to tell her who she is. Like Lou, you can come a long way too. You are not your trauma, your stress, or your overwhelming life events. Friends, as the musical group Avalon sings in "Where Joy and Sorrow Meet": "There is a place where hope remains in crowns of thorns and crimson stains." His name is Jesus!

Joy and sorrow meet at the cross of Jesus Christ. This is where we find hope and everlasting healing. Even if recovery doesn't happen 100 percent "this side of heaven," we believe and hold on to the words of Revelation 21:4 that promise, "'He will wipe every tear from their eyes. There will be no more death' or mourning or crying or pain, for the old order of things has passed away." I love how the New Living Translation ends this verse: "All these things are gone forever." *Forever.* May this promise of peace give you great hope! Let's move into part III, where we will work on reclaiming peace together.

PART III

RECLAIMING PEACE

"You have made us for yourself, O Lord,
and our hearts are restless until they rest in you."

Saint Augustine

CHAPTER 13

BEGIN AGAIN

"He heals the brokenhearted and binds up their wounds."

Psalm 147:3

How do you reclaim peace after trauma? What is the antidote for nagging worry, lack of trust, immobilizing fear, etc.? This chapter provides practical tips and information to help you manage issues such as sleepless nights, sorrow, and uncertainty about how to trust. You'll find a renewed sense of peace here. You can begin again.

ANN'S STORY

It was an evening like most others, typical for Ann since she had arrived in the Middle East. After dinner, and before she went to the third shift watch, she headed out for a quick and easy run in the cool evening before the sun set. She came to anticipate the evening routine, loved the gentle breeze on her face, feeling empowered by being in ideal physical shape. Ann ran inside the safe boundaries of the military base, and as usual, she wasn't alone on the gravel path. Tonight, there was only one other runner ahead of her. Ann didn't recognize the man, not from the back anyway. It didn't matter to her; she always felt more secure with others around.

With her earbuds in, listening to the latest Justin Bieber song pounding out an energetic beat, Ann started to quicken her pace. Her lungs resisted as she pushed herself harder than she had the night before. Focused on her breathing and stride, Ann was pleased to see that she was gaining on the soldier ahead. Aligning her breathing with the cadence of the song playing, she locked into a sweet spot, focused only on the few feet of the fine gravel path directly in front of her. That's when it happened—an event that would change her life forever.

Seconds after being thrown back and disoriented from the blast of an explosion, the thickness of smoke, and the burning smell, Ann realized an improvised explosive device had gone off when the footfall of the soldier running in front of her landed on it. She knew she couldn't waste any time if she wanted to save the man's life. With adrenaline kicking in, she raced to his side, knelt down, and tried to calm him while doing necessary triage to slow the bleeding. Although it didn't take long, everything felt in slow motion and the medic's arrival seemed to take forever. Watching them work and then as her comrade was being carried away on a stretcher, Ann sat in the dirt, hugging her knees to her chest, shaking and sobbing. What she had believed was safe, wasn't.

Her fellow soldier lost a limb but thankfully survived. Still, since that day many years ago, Ann has worried constantly. For her, this includes thinking intentionally and unintentionally about all the "what ifs" and "whys"—invisible demons that challenge her with questions like:

"What if you had gone running a few minutes earlier?"

"Why him, and not you?"

"What if you hadn't been there to help control his bleeding?"

"Why can't you just be grateful he survived and you weren't physically injured?" Well-meaning friends and family wanted to know too. Ann doesn't have an answer to give them. She knows this is survivor's guilt, but just because she knows what to name the source of her merciless thoughts doesn't mean the outcome will change.

Ann also struggles with anxiety, dreading the possibility of something bad happening again. It's hard for her to think of this long-ago tragedy as a onetime event that is rare and isolated in her life. Instead, she illogically fears the likelihood that something bad will happen at any moment. For years she's checked her locks repeatedly, she's never liked being in crowds or with strangers, and she frightens easily. She tried working in a local gift shop but couldn't tolerate the panic that filled her at the slightest trigger of the door banging open or sudden noises. Worry controlled Ann's life to the point that she had to stop working. Not working led to even more worry. Ann knew she had to do something to regain her life.

WORRY THAT CHOKES

How can we dare to move freely again after a tragedy? Excessive concern over a current or possible circumstance, and our lack of control, can take hold and trap us into ruminating, or staying stuck on repetitive thoughts. The reality is that *worry chokes us*. Worry can make us feel like we can't even breathe. In fact, Mark 4:19 says that worry chokes out the Word of God—the Truth. Jesus said this when He taught the parable of the sower.

From a boat on the lake, Jesus was teaching a crowd standing on the shore when He began talking to them about seeds. Using a metaphor they were familiar with, He explained that when the farmer throws out seeds, there are different responses to the seed. I imagine the crowd nodding. They knew the challenges of farming. To be clear, the seed Jesus spoke of is the Word of God. For some people, Jesus explained, Satan comes and takes away the life-giving seeds of God's Word. For others, "like seed sown on rocky places" (Mark 4:16), people can hear the Word, be filled with joy, but since no root takes place, they fall away. And for some people, the Word of God is "like seed sown among thorns" (verse 18) and *the worries of this life choke it* and make it unfruitful.

It's no coincidence that worriers feel as if they can't breathe and that many people who head to the hospital thinking they're having a heart attack are actually having a panic attack. When we worry, the Word of God cannot take root in our souls, and a life in His peace despite tribulations seems but a far-off wish or fantasy.

We are not seed makers, but we can till and soften our hearts and choose to allow the seeds of God's Word to plant deep and sprout within us. We can take in the sun and nutrients promised by the Holy Spirit to grow and thrive, planted by streams of water with our roots going deep into our Source of Life, rather than allowing old worry to continue choking us. This takes lots of practice and patience, especially for those who try and try to stop worrying but feel or believe they can't help it. What can we possibly hope for by inviting the gardener, God, to come and prune and free us from the tangle of weeds about us? Well, like apple trees in the sun, we can actively wait for the buds to appear and then the beautiful fruit of the Spirit to load our branches with: love, joy, peace, patience, kindness, goodness, faithfulness, gentleness, self-control (Galatians 5:22–23). It is possible to experience a reduction in worry.

CHELSEA'S STORY

Overcoming debilitating worry was grueling for Chelsea; although she didn't like to admit this, given her history in the United States Armed Forces. It's not easy for someone so tough to show what she perceived to be a weakness. Chelsea replayed the night in question over and over, desperately wishing that she had never accepted that drink from a stranger. He was a brother at arms, and she'd trusted him, until she woke up the next morning realizing she had been drugged and raped. Woozy and off-kilter, she couldn't recall many details from the night before. Stumbling to get dressed, she left the apartment she was brought to without seeing anyone else. She was thankful to make it out alive but was filled with a mixture of emotions ranging from numb disbelief to guilt and rage.

In the days and months that followed, Chelsea barely endured the rest of her enlistment. Between the shame and the unending sleepless nights, she was surprised she made it through at all. Walking around the military base became unbearable and meant she was met daily with familiar faces, of which at least one was the mask of her attacker. Who was it that had betrayed her, hurt her, in such a scheming act of violence? Chelsea kept her head down as much as possible, too embarrassed to run the risk of looking into the eyes of the man who had raped her.

At night, she tossed and turned, hating herself for the careless decision she'd made; she should have never been at the bar in the first place. She was exhausted beyond sanity but couldn't sleep. As soon as her eyes closed, her mind would fill with self-loathing and judgment: *What kind of idiot takes a drink from a stranger? How stupid could I be?* Her depression worsened. Only the alarm, the mess hall, the scheduled regimen kept her moving. *If I can just make it to the end of my enlistment, I can get away from this godforsaken place and start over.*

But starting over after getting out of the service proved more difficult than Chelsea expected. Living meant trusting again, and that was not going to happen. What she really wanted to do was curl up and sleep—forever. She was so, so tired. Chelsea moved into a house alone and covered all the windows with black drapes, blocking out every bit of sunlight and life from entering her home.

She lived meagerly off disability payments and rarely left home except to purchase groceries and go to medical appointments, when she'd put on a face long enough to get back home. Hope felt as elusive as winning the lottery.

Chelsea spent most days in bed watching TV and surfing the Internet, stuffing the dark abyss in her soul with food, when she had energy enough to eat. Depression consumed her until she was hardly able to lift her head, leaving little will to live. What was the point? No one seemed to know or care that she even existed. Each day she woke up hardly able to remember what happiness felt like, not knowing how she could go on like this, but not knowing how to change it either. "I hate my life!" she yelled at the dark ceiling.

One day Chelsea cracked open an eye and muscled up enough willpower to wrestle herself out of bed. She simply could not go on living this way. She would make one of her infrequent trips to the market, knowing it would take every ounce of energy she'd be able to muster up. While backing out of a parking space at the store, Chelsea heard a thump and then a scrape. Glancing into the rearview mirror, she saw that she'd backed into the shopping cart of a man loading his groceries into the SUV behind her. *Great. Now I can look forward to being sued.* She threw the car into park and jumped out to investigate the damage the cart had done to the SUV.

"I'm so sorry. Are you okay?"

"Chelsea?"

As it turns out, the man was Rob, a guy she'd dated briefly before enlisting. He'd been kind then. Maybe he still was.

"What can I do?" she asked, reaching for the bags still in the cart, as a way to avoid his eyes.

"Join me for dinner."

Uh, yeah, not going to happen. Chelsea glanced up and was surprised to see kindness. As it turned out, Rob was as decent as she remembered, and patient … and he was gently persistent with his invitation for dinner. Chelsea realized that she longed to have a friend in her life whom she could trust again. Rob hadn't give her any reason not to.

"What does he see in me—just a memory?" Chelsea asked her reflection in the mirror one day. Perhaps he only wanted to take advantage of her too. Her questions turned to one that loomed over her like a dark cloud threatening to storm: *How can I get from here back to trust?* She was terrified. Chelsea knew she was in no shape to start a romantic relationship, so she decided to do something about her condition. She dared to hope one more time.

For both Ann and Chelsea, loss had brought crippling injury to their bodies, souls, and minds. And even though they had begun healing, these moments of realizing how bad things had gotten and what they were missing out on in life led them to a necessary turning point. There came a moment when they knew they had to make a conscious choice to live again—to begin again—to intentionally take back their lives and get help. Ann and Chelsea both sought counseling from Christian therapists, which for them was a necessity to help traverse their way back to trust, finding courage through the Holy Spirit.

Peace is the antithesis to worry. Take a look at Ephesians 2:14–17 again:

> For he himself is our peace, who has made the two groups one and has destroyed the barrier, the dividing wall of hostility, by setting aside in his flesh the law with its commands and regulations. His purpose was to create in himself one new humanity out of the two, thus making peace, and in one body to reconcile both of them to God through the cross, by which he put to death their hostility. He came and preached peace to you who were far away and peace to those who were near.

Jesus is our peace. We are designed to have peace, to be at peace, and to spread peace because Jesus did not just talk about peace; rather, Christ's very essence and character *is* peace.

For some who have experienced trauma, as much as they want it to be the case, reading Scripture such as the verses above and praying for peace don't necessarily lead to peace. At least not immediately. And certainly not just by reading through the verses once or saying a quick prayer for peace. It can take much more time and effort than that. It takes courage. For some, it takes doing what Ann and Chelsea did: seeking mental health treatment where proven effective treatments can be utilized to help you work through difficult thoughts and feelings that are keeping you stuck. For anyone, it takes a willingness to be "tilled" and to receive the seeds of truth being sprinkled on our previously hard-rock soul. Despite tough circumstances, we embrace and take in the truth found in God's Word with an intentional deepening trust that peace *can come* and *only comes* through Jesus.

Ann was able to begin again. As a result of getting the help she needed, and being released *enough* from the chokehold of worry, she was able to go back to work part time. She still experiences some anxiety, but her moments of feeling totally overwhelmed have been manageable and much less frequent than before.

I love this quote from Corrie ten Boom: "Worry does not empty tomorrow of its worry, it empties today of its strength."[1] Jesus tells us there is no need to worry about tomorrow because tomorrow will worry about itself. Chelsea was able to begin again too. She found a safe place in counseling where she could ask her paralyzing questions and where she allowed much-needed healing to take place. Finally she was able to remove the dark shades from her windows and allow in light, both literally and figuratively. Eventually, she and Rob made many more trips to the fresh food market—together—and two years later, they married and started a family. Both women continue to work through the trauma they experienced. The journey hasn't been easy, but it has been worth it as they make daily decisions and do the hard work of getting their lives back. It is *never* too late to begin again.

CHAPTER 14

BREAKING THE CHAINS THAT KEEP US BROKEN

"Bear with each other and forgive one another if any of you has a grievance against someone. Forgive as the Lord forgave you."

Colossians 3:13

One of the most challenging and important steps in dealing with trauma, stress, and overwhelming life events is learning to forgive those who have harmed us. Forgiveness helps break the chains that keep us broken. This chapter offers practical steps and methods for forgiving others as well as accepting God's forgiveness for ourselves.

DIANA'S STORY

"I will *never* forgive him." With the punctuated emphasis of her angry words still hanging in the air, the visible reactions of the others sitting in the circle of sexual-trauma survivors varied from nods to frowns to tears. When I looked around the room, I also saw collective sadness, which meant the women attending the group exuded empathy. While it is completely understandable that this precious group member would not want to forgive her attacker, most of us knew **Diana's unwillingness to forgive was akin to holding her own head underwater.** In other words, she was holding herself back from healing.

I am not saying that people who perpetrate sexual crimes *deserve* to be forgiven. The fact is, many perpetrators couldn't care less about being forgiven, for a variety of reasons. Sometimes people who hurt others (which we all do to varying degrees) recognize the harm they've caused and attempt to make amends, but survivors certainly can't wait for an apology that may never come before setting themselves free through forgiveness.

You see, forgiveness is not a feeling; it is an intentional decision. It may not seem fair that you are asked to forgive someone who has used you, abused you, or worse, but hang in here while we unpack the power of forgiveness.

First, here are three challenging questions to ask yourself:

- Do I rehearse past aversive events?
- Do I harbor grudges?
- Do I entertain vengeful fantasies?

Times in your life when you cling to, and over which you justify your anger, are "unforgiven events." When we replay events from the past and allow ourselves to once again become angry, we are only punishing ourselves. Do you really want to give someone who has wronged you more power and control?

While your healing is not the ultimate meaning or purpose of forgiveness, releasing someone from your own judgment or vindication is the hinge upon which the door to your own freedom hangs. You don't forgive someone to release him or her from responsibility. You are certainly not excusing the action. You are not saying, "It's okay." (Don't ever say that. It's not okay that someone has wronged you.) What you *are* saying is yes to choosing to forgive so that you are no longer bound by anger and bitterness—so you can walk through that door to freedom.

WANDA'S STORY

Wanda grew up in a small town where everybody knew everybody. As a teenager, she was spending the night with a girl from school when the older brother of her friend sexually assaulted her. She never told anyone what happened, moved away after high school, and stuffed down the incident by abusing multiple substances.

Finally Wanda decided to get help and spent years in treatment for addiction to food and alcohol. She also worked extensively to recover from her traumatic event. She was actively taking her life back. Wanda was making good progress, right? Well, yes, but not entirely.

Two full decades after her assault, Wanda was back in her hometown visiting her father in the hospital. One day she came whipping around the corner of the cardio wing and ran squarely into the man who had violated her. At first Wanda wasn't sure it was him and chose to believe it wasn't. She didn't need this. Not now. Not ever. But it was him and he too happened to have a parent in the hospital. There he was—the man who'd wrecked her life—a man who was beloved by his small-town community.

Running into her perpetrator sent Wanda into a tailspin, and after several days of crazy, she called the man's home and told his wife what he had done to her. No one in her parents' town believed her. Not this upstanding leader who served on city council, coached Little League, and rescued kittens out of trees! To say this retraumatization set her recovery back is an understatement.

As a therapist, I am often asked by clients if they should confront someone who hurt them. While it is never my job to tell them yes or no, I do help them explore their options thoroughly instead of making a rash decision. Wanda made her decision to confront her attacker and his wife on her own and without any support. In fact, when her father found out, he got upset with Wanda and told her she should have left the past alone.

Oh, it pains me so much to think of Wanda addressing this issue by herself, but she wanted this man to acknowledge what he had done. She wanted an apology too. She had been waiting for decades. Sadly, she would keep on waiting because he never intended to risk his reputation by admitting his wrongdoing. I can't say how she would have reacted if she had forgiven him before running into him that fateful day in the county hospital. But for Wanda, the *experience she had as a teenager was an unforgiven event that continued to cause her endless pain.* As incredibly difficult as it may be, Wanda can choose to forgive her attacker and, in doing so, release herself from the iron grip she's allowed him to hold on her all these years. She can take hold of the power of forgiveness and find emotional relief. You can too.

BECAUSE GOD FORGAVE FIRST

As wonderful as emotional freedom is, forgiveness is not only for our own relief. We are asked to forgive because we have been forgiven by God, and because God calls us to forgive others. In fact, when Peter asked Jesus how many times he was expected to forgive someone who sinned against him, Jesus told him to forget about the seven times Peter mentioned and to forgive seventy-seven times (Matthew 18:21–22). My pastor, Dr. J., puts it this way: "Jesus was telling Peter to stop counting and keep on forgiving." We are asked to forgive regardless of the sin or frequency of sin that someone committed against God … or us.

I don't know about you, but at first glance this sounds impossible and even absurd. Such an expectation runs entirely contrary to what we know to be right. I think of the woman whose husband has cheated on her, who has to face him and the new "love of his life" every time she begrudgingly hands off the kids for his visitation—knowing he'll stuff them full of junk food and give them limitless access to television and computers before sending them back overly exhausted and irritable. Forgive him after what he did to me? Forgive him over and over? I don't think so! Yeah, it sounds impossible. And absurd. But let's keep going before we write this whole forgiveness thing off.

WHAT DESERVES FORGIVENESS

A theological debate abounds as to whether God ranks sin. We know that the "wages of sin is death"; however, Romans 6:23 doesn't say that the wages of adultery is death. It doesn't say the wages of lying is death. Or stealing. Or gluttony. Or even murder. Nope. The Bible simply says *sin*. This is, in my opinion, the best case for God not ranking sin. At the same time, we also know that the earthly consequences vary depending on the sin.

When I was a little girl, I was kind of a mess. One summer, I was looking for ways to entertain myself and sneaked around the side of the house to play in my dad's big, old Mercury that was parked in the driveway. The car was hot and smelled like leather, so I rolled down the window and imagined being all grown up. I pretended I was driving the car over to our neighbor Mrs. Christopher's house for candy and a chat about her time in Europe. That's when I discovered that not only could I reach the pedals with the tips of my shoes by sliding all the way to the edge of the seat, but I was even able to shift the gears (this car was made before manufacturers installed a mechanism to prevent vehicles from shifting when the car is off).

I got bored easily, so after a few minutes of that I hopped out of the car and ran away to the next adventure. Before long, we heard honking coming from the street. Boy was I surprised when

I saw my dad's car sitting at a strange angle in the street blocking both lanes of traffic. Apparently, I had put the car in reverse and jumped out before it started to roll.

When I broke the rule and played in my dad's car, my consequences were far different than when I called 911 just to see what would happen and then ran and hid in the back of my mom's station wagon waiting to see the results. I did wrong both times, but my parents were able to see the difference between my actions in both events. I did break the rules in the first example, and was disciplined for my actions. But in the second scenario, I did something *intentionally wrong*, which resulted in a worse outcome for everyone.

Back to forgiveness. God offers us forgiveness, and we are asked to forgive others too. In the book of Matthew, we find Jesus teaching about praying in quiet humility. There He teaches us how to pray the Lord's Prayer, wherein the old laws of "an eye for an eye" no longer apply. Jesus addresses God as Father, an intimate relational gesture, instead of looking at God as only judge, and teaches us that under the law of grace we are to be mindful of our own sin and debts and trespasses; we are asked then to release those who've wronged us. Matthew 6:14–15 reads: "For if you forgive other people when they sin against you, your heavenly Father will also forgive you. But if you do not forgive others their sins, your Father will not forgive your sins." These verses are not saying that if you don't forgive someone, then you are not saved.[1] The scripture is most likely saying that relationship breaks down and you cannot be in daily communion with God your loving Father if you are not willing to forgive others.

In response to these challenging verses in Matthew, GotQuestions.org explains, "Any sin committed against us, no matter how terrible, is trivial in comparison to our sins against God." Though it's tough to contemplate, God's Word stakes the claim, and therefore, it is without error. While no one is expected to *instantly* forgive those who bring pain, and while some trespasses and debts take much longer to recover from than others, it is critical that we all understand the importance of forgiveness. Only then can we be more free, more at peace, and closer to God. The truth is that in order to heal, we forgive. In order to be right with God, we forgive. And believe it or not, we can even develop *empathy* for those who have harmed us.

WALKING THAT MILE

Empathy can be a challenging concept, especially in relation to extending mercy to one who's brought hardship or suffering. *Empathy* is not to be confused with *sympathy*, which is feeling sorry for someone. It's interesting to me that when a loved one dies, we send a sympathy card to the family. For most of us, although we are sorry for their loss, we also have empathy because we too have experienced loss. That's what empathy is all about: being able to put oneself in another's shoes. Having empathy for another person doesn't necessarily mean you have experienced what he or she has endured, and it doesn't mean you are excusing any of that person's wrong behaviors. Empathy is a necessary way to connect; it's a reminder that we are all human.

When I worked with clients whose behaviors were clearly harmful to themselves or others, it was empathy that allowed me to work with some of the worst offenders. I love the expression "There but for the grace of God go I," because it reminds me that we are all on the same continuum of sin and all are capable of slipping and falling into Satan's deception. We are all capable of hurting others. And if I remember that, to God, all sin is worth death, and we are all sinners, then I am able to see the person sitting in front of me as a human being created in the image of God rather than an adulterer, an abuser, or a pedophile.

I wonder if it's possible for you to put yourself in the shoes of someone who wronged you. Were you abused by a parent who "disciplined" you in the same way she or he was "disciplined"? Was your best friend killed in front of you by the enemy—who shot before being shot at? Has a good friend turned away from you, perhaps because you are a reflection of what she doesn't have or what she wants to be? I've known people in all of these situations, and I can tell you that, as difficult as it is, empathy is possible.

Make no mistake, **being able to empathize with someone is not intended to excuse that person.** And forgiving another does not mean you can or should trust them again either. Forgiveness also does not necessarily mean reconciliation. Trust and reconciliation are absolutely dependent on each individual situation. For example, I've known people who had a spouse involved in an affair, yet they were able to recover from this experience, rebuild trust, and reconcile as a couple. I've also known those who've had a spouse involved in an affair, and the redevelopment of trust and reconciliation never took place, sometimes because the offending spouse left. Many varying factors come into play in both scenarios, and the recovery from the adultery was dependent on these factors.

We learn in Daniel 9:9 that "the LORD our God is merciful and *forgiving*." Ephesians 1:7 tells us that in Him, we have redemption through His blood and the *forgiveness* of sins. As Christians, we can believe in 1 John 1:9, "If we confess our sins, he is faithful and just and will forgive us our sins and purify us from all unrighteousness." We may not be stellar at this business of forgiving, but we can trust that the work has already been started for us. Pursuing right relationship with God and what He desires is the right thing. Since forgiveness is so clearly what God wants, we can be sure this is right. I'll boldly ask: Are you willing to forgive those who have hurt you?

FORGETTING

In addition to our undeserved forgiveness, God *forgets* our wrongdoings. In Psalm 103:12, we are told that God removes our transgressions as far as the east is from the west. And in three separate places (Isaiah 43:25; Hebrews 8:12; Hebrews 10:17), the Bible says God will not remember our sins. Wow. But God is God, and we are mere humans. We can't possibly forget, right? We might get angry at the mere suggestion—unless we want to walk, or even run(!), free of the chains and prisons of the past.

I am not sure our human minds are capable of forgetting serious inflictions made upon us, but I do believe we are invited to team with Jesus in our desire to do so. When we focus our eyes on Jesus and the amazing work He is doing in our lives and in the lives of others, we become filled with gratitude. The miracle of forgetting begins when we daily fill our minds with the beautiful truth of who God is. As we focus our sight on Christ's unspeakable love for us, the past begins to fade and we can get through an hour or maybe two without thinking about the trauma. I've seen it happen many times. As love and healthy relationships start to fill your life, one day you might even wake up and realize you went an entire day, maybe more, without thinking about past offenses, without weeping.

You are becoming free. Free indeed (John 8:36). This is why God instructs us, His children, to forgive (read Matthew 6:14–15). It stems from God's pure love for us. Some goals of forgiveness are to let go of the offense and offender so *you* can lead an emotionally stable life focused on the present, develop the ability to have a good life despite past wounds, and achieve compassion toward others. It takes tremendous strength to forgive someone or something that you believe has wronged you, so let's review some benefits of forgiveness:

1. Resolving pain from an old wound.
2. Releasing long-held anger that interferes with emotional well-being.
3. Expressing anger appropriately instead of misdirecting it at others or yourself.

4. Less depression and anxiety, more joy and peace.

5. Personal empowerment.

6. Most importantly, rightness with God.

A PRACTICAL HOW-TO

One method that can help kick-start forgiveness is to write a letter to someone you are angry with. However, think carefully before sending the letter. You may find that the person on the receiving end does not believe he or she needs to be forgiven and your letter could make the situation worse. Try to be as empathic toward the person as you would want him or her to be toward you. And, if the Lord leads you to send the letter, then send it. If not, you can destroy the letter in such a way that it helps bring some closure (such as burning or burying it). These types of actions signify getting rid of the pain contained within the letter. And, again, if you need professional help in this process, don't be afraid to seek it out.

FORGIVING ME

Dear ladies, as much as I hope you will consider forgiving others, it is equally important to forgive yourself. You may believe you are not worthy of forgiveness. Perhaps you even think you deserve your pain and punish yourself. But will the punishment ever be enough? In chapter 8 we discussed how one particular face of frustration (anger) is *a mask for shame*. What would it require to forgive yourself and give up the shame you feel? Ask yourself these questions:

- What core value was broken as a result of your past experiences?
- How has this damaged your self-worth?
- How have you punished yourself?
- Will the punishment ever be enough?

The goal of these questions—to help you forgive yourself, release long-held shame, reduce anger, and build hope—is the impetus for breaking free enough to move toward others again. I'm reminded of this clumsy, yet beautiful image of forgiveness as a dance, as described by L. Gregory Jones:

> We need the support, encouragement and discerning help of others as we learn how to practice forgiveness in every aspect of our lives. Learning the alternative life-way of forgiveness takes time and involves hard work.... It happens as we are transformed by walking in this way of life with other people, in response to God's active presence among us. The process of forgiveness begins as we venture forth, either on our own or through the invitation of others, to learn the steps of this beautiful, if sometimes awkward, dance.[2]

We find many verses in the Bible that speak on the topic of the dance of forgiveness, of releasing one's past sin. One of my favorites is Colossians 3:13. It reads, "Bear with each other and forgive one another if any of you has a grievance against someone. Forgive as the Lord forgave you."

What is your favorite verse on the topic of forgiveness? Write it out here *and* on a note card that you can carry with you as a reminder to forgive.

_____

_____

_____

What does it mean for you to "reclaim peace"? Forgiving yourself may be even more difficult than forgiving others. God forgives. God forgets. God is filled with mercy and grace toward us, and He is the authority on all of this, so we can certainly trust Him. Try showing a little bit of that kindness to yourself.

Some believe the anger of God railed against humanity in such severe force that it drove nails through the hands and feet of Jesus. But nothing could be further from the truth. "Love, not anger," says author Richard Foster, "brought Jesus to the cross … Jesus knew that by His suffering He could actually absorb all the evil of humanity and so heal it, forgive, redeem it."[3] And He did just that.

Reclaiming sanity in large part comes when we can put on the mind of Christ, allowing Truth to erase old broken beliefs and bust open old rusting prison doors, breaking the chains that make and keep us broken and crippled. With His death and resurrection, Jesus purchased renewed innocence. Because of this we can glimpse again our heritage, our beginnings, and hope for a future. Forgiveness clears the debris out of the path leading to our pure and holy God, and then to ourselves and others. When we choose to forgive, sadness and pain will stop in as guests from time to time, but these emotions don't get to take up permanent residence as housemates. We can forgive others, and we can forgive ourselves. And, sometimes, we can rebuild relationships.

CHAPTER 15

REBUILDING RELATIONSHIPS

"All this is from God, who reconciled us to himself through Christ and gave us the ministry of reconciliation."

2 Corinthians 5:18

You're working on forgiveness. Now, what do you do about the relationships that are damaged as a result of past negative experiences? In this chapter, you'll learn how to be empathetic toward people you are angry with or hurt by, and start to rebuild relationships with those who have been negatively affected by the consequences of your negative emotions and behaviors, which are a result of your trauma, stress, or overwhelming life events. You'll also be encouraged to share with others your story and the impact (not necessarily details) of your trauma as a way of establishing and rebuilding trust.

Forgiveness is about coming together again, restoring relationships that can be healthy and vibrant and alive. We may never understand the past and its pain, and not everyone will live in harmony. After all, humanity's love, at best, is broken. Even when we desire and strive to love perfectly, we disappoint and hurt people. This is why we are so dependent on our relationship with God first and foremost. Though anger feels better and more justified at times, we choose to forgive because we've been forgiven. We love because we are loved. And while we have limited human forgiveness to offer, Jesus promises to do the rest even as our offender(s) in their clumsy gait bump up against the tender spots of our wounds.

Not only is God the source of our healing and the restorer of broken hearts, He teaches us how to love anew. This is why we turn again and again to our master and redeemer, perfect love Himself, Jesus. Only when we experience such love can we heal from the pain of relational bruises and begin pursuing and participating in wholesome relationships.

BELINDA'S STORY

Belinda had a difficult upbringing. She didn't realize until adulthood that her mother, June, had experienced a lot of anxiety and depression while being a single mom on the run from an alcoholic husband and raising her three daughters. Belinda wished her mom had been more open with her about the hard times of their past. She longed for a closer relationship with her mom and thought understanding her mom's emotional problems might have helped them to bond.

Belinda had begun having her own problems, and when she couldn't bear the weight of her negative emotions alone anymore, she went to her mom and poured out her heart. June listened with a stoic expression. After a long pause, she said, "I wanted to protect you girls from this …" and then the dam she'd been holding all those years began to crumble as she revealed through a river of tears all the suffering she'd endured as a result of her own frightening thoughts and feelings.

Belinda could relate all too well to the nightmares, panic attacks, and crying jags June disclosed. This revelation helped start the process of rebuilding their relationship. Belinda learned that it was better to share than to stuff emotions as she began to relate to her mother in a way she never had before.

Two types of relationships may need to be rebuilt as a result of your trauma. The first type includes relationships with *those who have harmed you*, similar to Belinda's story; and the second type includes relationships with *those who are being negatively affected as a result of your present reactions to your past experiences*. In this chapter, we'll explore both types and what you can do to start rebuilding your relationships.

REBUILDING WITH THE PERSON WHO HURT YOU

Of course, we know harm takes place to varying degrees, and our reactions to this harm are just as varied. Does forgiveness always mean reconciliation? Christian theologians have debated the complexity of reconciliation for centuries. I believe reconciliation is biblical, and a wonderful goal, if and when it is possible. Yet I recognize it's not always possible.

A dear friend was abused by a parent. She maintains a healthy distance from this individual, yet she does continue to honor her parent, as she takes this commandment very seriously. How? She maintains appropriate boundaries and spends limited amounts of time with this parent. It is difficult because it means she does not get to see other family members she loves as often, but she has to take this step in order to protect herself emotionally and maintain stability. While she has forgiven her parent for the past abuse, she rightfully does not allow the abuse to continue. For her, this is what reconciliation looks like. As L. Gregory Jones noted, "Sometimes reconciliation requires separation, particularly in abusive or oppressive situations where proximity threatens our very identities in relation to God…. Boundaries are legitimate. Permanent hopeless barriers are not."[1]

RECONCILIATION

Remember how we noted the various degrees of harm and various degrees of reactions to harm? The same is true for reconciliation. It may mean that the relationship is fully restored. Say, for example, you are the adult child of a recovering alcoholic. Perhaps you have been able to forgive and reconcile with your now sober parent, and you enjoy having a healthy relationship. As a result of the actions of both parties, the relationship is fully restored.

Reconciliation may also mean the relationship is partially restored. An example of this would be an adult child forgiving a parent who was not around while they were growing up, and being able to have a relationship of sorts (perhaps some visits or phone calls, with caution).

Finally, reconciliation may be minimally restored. This is where my friend fits in. She respects her parent and sees this parent about once a year. Sadly, but realistically, some relationships can never be restored (and some should never be restored unless the abusive party receives extensive treatment and demonstrates significant change). Remember that sometimes we choose to forgive those we will never see again, someone who has died, a huge and powerful institution that destroyed our livelihood, or an attacker whose face we never saw. Wrote Lewis B. Smedes in his book that has become a classic work on forgiving hurts we don't deserve, "We cannot breathe back all the old life; we forgive and reunite on the terms that time and circumstance make available to us."[2]

You may be asking, "Where do I even begin?" I would suggest you start by determining which relationships you desire to be restored. It may be that you want to reconcile with someone who chooses not to reunite with you. This happened to someone else I know. She was adopted as an infant and longed to meet her birth mother. After decades of searching, she located her birth mother only to find out her birth mother did not want to have any contact. Soon after, her birth mother died, and she had to accept and cope with the fact that she would never meet her birth mother while on earth. Her hope is that her birth mother was saved and she will meet her in heaven. Although it's sad and difficult, we have to accept that reconciliation doesn't always happen. And certainly not always in the manner we desire.

It may be that someone from a broken past relationship wants to reconcile with you but you are simply not capable of or willing to be a part of his or her life. While working on forgiveness, you may recognize you cannot be healthy and continue to interact. Accept this. Trust yourself. If both you and the other person want to resolve a past offense peacefully, you have a common goal to work toward. Sometimes this can happen just between the two of you; other times counseling may be needed.

I recall a man and woman who came to see me for counseling. It took me a couple of sessions before I figured out they were friends and not in a romantic relationship. We all had a chuckle once I realized this. It may be rare, but some friendships are worth seeking professional help over. Typically, friendships can find health and forgiveness or be dissolved without professional intervention. But, certainly, relationships such as parent-child and spouses can benefit greatly from these types of services.

If you're not sure whether the other person wants to share life again, or whether the relationship can be reconciled, you may consider reaching out to that person you're missing. While in many instances a face-to-face or phone conversation is best, writing a letter might be a better choice in other situations. This would allow you to think carefully about what you want to say and not have to run the risk of sitting face to face or voice to voice with someone who may reject a reunion.

REBUILDING WITH SOMEONE WHO FEELS HURT BY YOU

Dealing with trauma, stress, or overwhelming life events could mean there is a period of time when your focus on healing may seem selfish to others. In reality, it's not selfish because your intention is to become a healthier person who is more capable of having flourishing relationships. At the same time, if you are so caught up in yourself that you ignore your loved ones and their needs, you run the serious risk of losing them—emotionally or physically.

Saint Francis of Assisi said we should seek to understand rather than to be understood. If you're like me, you are used to sharing your own opinion (frequently), but maybe you're not as accustomed to listening to others. Proverbs 18:2 says that "fools find no pleasure in understanding but delight in airing their own opinions." Undoubtedly, this negatively affects our relationships. The phrase attributed to Saint Francis has been made popular among corporate leaders and those who are proactively learning how to communicate for success in their businesses and families, but the same timeless wisdom applies to rebuilding relationships after trauma as well.

Have *your* relationships been affected by your inability to see beyond your own pain? Perhaps you are not able to recognize how your loved ones experience your negative emotions or behaviors. Maybe you lash out at your kids without realizing it. Or your husband feels rejected because you no longer have time for him. Perhaps you are too stressed out or overwhelmed and you're just not emotionally available for others. Should your loved ones suffer as a result? It may be helpful to learn how to empathize with them. Yes, here is the concept of empathy again. Not only is empathy necessary in forgiving, but the ability to put yourself in someone else's shoes also allows you to reset the framework for building a bridge back to those you love.

How do your loved ones experience you and share life with you?

Empathizing with someone who has been traumatized is not always easy. It might be helpful if *you* know and understand how other people experience your emotional states. One way to find out is by conducting an empathic interview. This is when you sit down with someone in your life and ask specific questions. As a result, you might be more motivated to heal and change. The better able you are to understand how others experience you, the healthier your relationships can be. Warning: this activity is tough … and just might change your life.

THE EMPATHIC INTERVIEW

Select a loved one with whom your relationship needs work and ask him or her the following questions (rule number one during this process: listen and do not react):

> 1. How do I appear to you, emotionally? For example, do I seem frustrated, sad, lonely, angry?
> 2. How do you feel toward me?
> 3. Do you feel close to me or distant from me?

Now that you have this information, what can you do with it? You can choose to continue putting up walls of defense and further damaging meaningful relationships, or you can work toward repairing your relationships. How? First of all, put yourself in your interviewee's place for a minute and try to feel what he or she must be feeling. This is true empathy. From that place, you can take responsibility and acknowledge that your actions, emotions, moods, or words have had an impact on your loved one. Then if you really want to repair the relationship, you can make a commitment to address your negative symptoms so that your actions, emotions, moods, and words communicate love instead of pain.

GINA'S STORY

Gina and her husband came to see me because, although she wanted to be intimate with her husband, she struggled with desire. Their marriage had gotten to the point to where each night she went into the bathroom to change into baggy, long-sleeve flannel pajamas to signal to her husband that, no, they were not going to be intimate that night either. He was growing more frustrated, wondering what he had done to drive her away and what he could do to help her desire return.

In counseling, Gina shared that a recent event had triggered her memories of past sexual abuse, and she became anxious about putting herself in the vulnerable position of being intimate with her husband. Gina's past was greatly affecting her present and damaging her marriage. Once they were in counseling and able to open up, he became more sensitive to her and wanted to be supportive while she worked on addressing deeply rooted wounds that had never completely healed over. For Gina, this process ripped open old scars, and she needed to do a lot of work to heal—including working on her overall relationship with her husband.

Dr. James "Jim" Sells and his colleague Dr. Mark Yarhouse wrote a book titled *Counseling Couples in Conflict: A Relational Restoration Model*. Early in the book, they address the importance of "Becoming US in a culture of ME."[3] The most poignant point, in my opinion, is that the "us" needs to be elevated in order for healing to be a possibility. There must be a unity, and in marriages a true "two will become one" (Ephesians 5:31) approach in order for that relationship to be healthy and thrive. At the same time, each individual's needs should not be ignored. Sells and Yarhouse explain that moving away from selfishness means that while the ME (as opposed to less selfish "me") identity of a person "isn't suppressed, squelched, or disregarded, it is voluntarily placed aside in order to participate in a greater good."[4]

Gina discovered that she appeared irritable and fearful toward her husband and that he, in turn, was starting to resent her. While he wanted to be close again, he had begun to mirror his wife's actions of pulling away. When Gina recognized that not only was she suffering but her husband and their marriage were too, she was motivated to address these issues. I have seen this time and again through the empathic interview. Seeing a dispute from another's perspective can heavily influence how we look at a situation or react to it.

In his book *Strength to Love*, Martin Luther King Jr. wrote, "Love is the only force capable of transforming an enemy into a friend. We never get rid of an enemy by meeting hate with hate; we get rid of an enemy by getting rid of enmity. By its very nature, hate destroys and tears down; by its very nature, love creates and builds up. Love transforms with redemptive power."[5] We choose love, either by closing the gap between us and the one who hurt us, or by reconciling with those we continue to harm with our own residual pain. We reclaim peace while rebuilding relationships as Gina began to do—and also while telling our story as Belinda did.

Are you ready to work on restoring your relationships? Once you decide which one to focus on first, and regardless if it is possible, you can begin the hard work of reconciliation. Part of this will include addressing and working through conflict. We'll look at various methods of problem solving and conflict resolution in the next chapter.

Meanwhile, I encourage you to share your story. To not be ashamed. To share instead of stuffing. To reconcile. Each time we tell the story of our redemption, light shines in where there were only murky shadows, and truth breaks chains of secrecy.

CHAPTER 16

SOLVING PROBLEMS IN A MINDFUL WAY

"Set your mind on things above, not on earthly things."
Colossians 3:2

This chapter contains three useful models: the conflict-resolution model, the five steps of problem solving, and the cost-benefit analysis. All have similarities and differences and give you opportunities to determine what works best for you as you work on solving your most difficult problems.

By taking a mindful approach to daily life, we don't have to experience so many negative emotions and allow the little (and big) clashes to lead us down a path we don't want to go. We can intentionally solve problems, resolve conflict, and find inner peace.

What is a mindful approach? Being *mindful* means being present, composed, and pausing before reacting to life's challenges.[1] Let me share a story that may illustrate this.

Margo was in a city she had never visited before and was on her way from the airport to her hotel. When she arrived and went to check in, she realized she had taken the wrong shuttle. Consequently, she had arrived at a lovely hotel, but not the one with her reservation. Graciously, the concierge offered transport for her to the correct location. Even while waiting for an hour on the heels of an exhausting day of travel, Margo reminded herself, "I will choose not to be irritated with myself or others over this. Yes, I have an early engagement in the morning, but nothing tragic happened. I am here safe and sound, and I will get plenty of rest before my event starts. Today is a good day!"

Wouldn't it be wonderful if we all talked to ourselves like this when things didn't go perfectly? This is being mindful.

FOLLOWING JESUS AT THE SHORE

The breeze on my face was warm that day when I stood on the shore of the Sea of Galilee. I'd just sailed around that beautiful sea on what local guides affectionately called "The Jesus Boat." To be in the very place where spectacular biblical events such as Jesus and Peter walking on water are believed to have taken place was surreal, and I had to keep telling myself that I was really there. As I walked along the shore looking for seashells and watching the fishermen, I thought of what it must have been like during the time of Jesus.

The Bible became more alive than ever for me. I looked out at the backdrop of the story of Peter doubting Jesus's ability to keep him walking on water. How interesting it is that the New Testament points out numerous times how little faith Jesus's followers had. If the disciples who were *with Jesus physically* had fear and doubt, it is no surprise that we do too.

In the aftermath of trials and troubles, our tendency is to react or to pull away with doubt or fear, yet we can walk in freedom. Being prayerfully attentive means to see with spiritual eyes rather than through our flesh. This doesn't mean we will never worry again or that we will never be afraid again. Still, we can commit ourselves to being true followers of Christ, accepting that life will not be perfect and trusting Him even when times are tough. God can handle our pain. Remember, Jesus said to cast our cares on Him because His yoke is easy and His burden is light (Matthew 11:30). Imagine taking all the junk that robs you of rest and steals your joy and handing it over. What does that mean for you?

You don't have to solve your disputes alone. In fact, the Bible teaches us a lot about how to address conflict. In Matthew 18:15, we are told to go directly to a fellow Christian. In this context, it is not just about a sin against *you*. When anyone in the body of Christ is wounded, the whole body suffers. I believe these same principles can be applied when you have been wronged. All through the Gospels we see Jesus moving toward others, removing any obstacle that might stand in the way of unity, of reconciling and forgiving. Jesus is our master teacher, our model to follow when we need to confront another person who has caused upset.

Where do you find much-needed answers when seeing red? If you daily read the Gospels and the timeless wisdom found in Proverbs, and you hide these truths in your heart, your first response to being wronged will be sourced there. Then you'll know to prayerfully explore the situation and be prepared to address it in a grace-filled and reasonable manner. Life is difficult and messy and we need to proceed with great care.

Dilemmas come in all shapes and sizes and often result in needless pain. I often think that I *like* human beings well enough; it's just that getting along with them can be difficult! As long as we are the only one in the room, we're not being at all selfish or crabby; we're not using a "tone" or giving someone the "eye" (you know the look—the one your mama had that would have you six feet under if looks could kill). Put one other person in here with us and all of a sudden two opinions are present, two ways of seeing who to vote for, how to best get a project done at work, or even what to have for dinner, and *boom!* Conflict.

Because negative emotions narrow our view, the blinders need to be removed so we see all the potential solutions to the problem. Is it possible that you are not as "right" as you think you are? (Hey, it's happened to me!) In the remainder of this chapter, we will explore a variety of methods to address and resolve conflicts or problems. Below are three models you can tailor to fit. These include: (1) the conflict-resolution model, (2) the five stages of effective problem solving, and (3) the cost-benefit analysis.[2] Try them out; they just might bring a new breakthrough for you.

THE CONFLICT-RESOLUTION MODEL

I like the conflict-resolution model because it syncs nicely with Christ's teaching in Matthew 18:15: "If your brother or sister sins, go and point out their fault, just between the two of you. If they listen to you, you have won them over." The question is how to go about doing this kindly and gently. Consider thinking through the following steps before approaching your brother or sister (fellow believer in Christ), keeping in mind that "winning one over" does not equate with scoring against an opponent—just like a body, a family, marriage, or friendship is not two opposing teams. If the eye accidentally gets poked by the pointer finger, the finger doesn't defend itself or brag about points won. No, it comforts the eye.

With the conflict-resolution model, you are identifying a problem and the impact of the problem. You are also making a decision as to whether this is a problem you want to attempt to resolve. (Like my mama always told me, "Pick your battles." Decide who you want to tangle with, and do so carefully.) If this is an issue you cannot or should not ignore, you will work toward resolution.

1. Identify the problem causing the conflict.
2. Identify the feelings associated with the conflict.
3. Identify the impact of the problem causing the conflict.
4. Through prayer and reflection, discern whether to attempt to resolve the conflict.

5. Work for resolution of the conflict:

   a. How would you like the problem to be resolved?

   b. How will you attempt to resolve the problem? (If you aren't sure, look at the next activity.)

   c. Attempt to resolve the problem.

FIVE STEPS OF EFFECTIVE PROBLEM SOLVING

In addition to the conflict-resolution model, there is another great plan for solving problems using five simple steps. When I used this with my anger management groups, it was actually fun and funny, believe it or not. Try these steps for yourself:

1. Determine if you have a problem. (Ask yourself questions such as: Do I have negative emotions? Is my heart racing? Am I having trouble breathing? Am I having bad thoughts? Am I yelling, crying, hitting, or demonstrating any other negative or harmful behaviors?)

2. If yes, then define the problem:

- Separate facts from opinion. Avoid assuming you know what someone else is thinking or feeling. Unless and until the person tells you, this is just your opinion. Instead of jumping to conclusions, take some time to collect the facts first.

- Separate the person from the problem. For example, you may be upset with a friend for canceling last minute on the scheduled lunch that you had been looking forward to for weeks and had secured childcare for. Instead of thinking the worst about your friend, notice the behavior that upset you and recognize the emotion it triggered in you (in this case, perhaps the feeling of abandonment came up).

3. Brainstorm all possible solutions. Don't leave anything out! This can be entertaining as you think of every possible solution. Use your creativity here and don't hold anything back. Using the previous example, some solutions would be to get angry with your friend, to stop speaking to her, to yell at her, to be empathetic toward her, to use "I" statements (such as "I am hurt") to let her know how you feel, to discuss the issues that led to her canceling, to not schedule with her again when you would need childcare, etc. You will likely find that you can use more than one solution. Which of these solutions do you think are the best options for the health of your relationship?

4. Look at your options in a realistic manner: only keep options that will help you achieve your goal without creating new problems.

5. Try the solutions. If none of the solutions work, go back to step 2 and see if you need to redefine the problem.

COST-BENEFIT ANALYSIS

The third option to solving disputes is the cost-benefit analysis (CBA),[3] which asks you to identify not only what triggered the opposition but also *what belief* led up to it. You have some experience evaluating beliefs from back in chapter 11 on intense emotions. After listing the situation and belief, you will think through the short-term and long-term costs and benefits of your negative emotions and resulting behaviors. We know that, generally speaking, "cost" is what we pay for something. But in this context the word carries even more weight. According to Merriam-Webster's, it is the "expenditure made to achieve an object," *as well as* "loss or penalty incurred especially in gaining something."[4] Merriam-Webster's second definition of *benefit* is most applicable to this exercise: "something that promotes well-being" or is "a useful aid." After going through each step in the cost-benefit analysis, you can decide whether the costs (consequences) or the benefits are greater.

Let's play out a scenario. When Hannah came to me for counseling, we worked through several battles she and her family were fighting at home. One battle looked like this:

Dr. Shaler: What is the problem situation?

Hannah: *My children's constant arguing raises my stress level. I begin to feel overwhelmed, and when I can't deal with them anymore I lash out at them in anger.*

Dr. Shaler: What is your belief about the problem?

Hannah: *Children should not argue, at least not incessantly like mine do. Parents should be able to prevent their children from arguing.*

When they argue, I should be able to calmly and patiently discipline them so they will not argue.

Dr. Shaler: What are your negative emotions and behaviors?

Hannah: *I feel angry so I yell. Then I feel guilty and regret yelling.*

Sometimes it helps to have a visual. When we put Hannah's responses on the white board, they looked like this:

Benefits	**Costs**
Short-term benefits	*Short-term costs*
When I yell at my kids, they stop fighting.	My kids are hurt by my action.
	I feel guilt and regret.
	My blood pressure goes up.
Long-term benefits	*Long-term costs*
There are none.	I'm damaging the relationship with my children.
	I'm causing myself health problems.

HANNAH'S STORY

When Hannah recognized how she was harming herself, her children, and their relationship, she was no longer willing to continue in the same pattern. By breaking the situation down using the cost-benefit analysis, she was able to see what to change and she chose to write it out as a reminder of what she needed to do to minimize her negative emotions and behaviors and replace them with positive ones. Instead of continuing in the habit of yelling at her children, she talked with them about everyone taking a time-out, herself included. This allowed everyone time to calm down and gave Hannah an opportunity to think through her reactions instead of jumping to overreacting, as had become her routine. With this simple, mindful change, Hannah's family experienced remarkable benefits.

Your turn. Fill out the below cost-benefit analysis using your own real-life situation.

Problem situation?

_____

_____

Belief about the problem?

_____

_____

Benefits   **Costs**

Short-term benefits   *Short-term costs*

1. _____   _____

2. _____   _____

3. _____   _____

Long-term benefits   *Long-term costs*

1.) _____   _____

2.) _____   _____

3.) _____   _____

How has this exercise helped you?

_____

_____

MINDFULNESS AT ANOTHER LEVEL

Now that you know three ways to resolve problems, let's take mindfulness to another level. We'll start by going back to Israel. Close your eyes and imagine you went to sleep, and upon waking, you are in Israel. You're standing on the sandy shore of the Sea of Galilee, the warmth of the sun on your face. As you stand where Jesus stood, pause for a moment. What do you hear? What do you smell? Look around; what do you see? What are you thinking? Perhaps if you squint you can see Jesus a short distance away. You see a slight movement and realize He's walking toward you, as a friend would whom you haven't seen for some months, His arms open wide, beckoning, waiting to wrap you in a tight embrace. "Come to me, daughter. I will give you rest." You run to Him, sobbing, and throw yourself in His arms. Your burden begins to lift and you feel the weight in your chest lift. You stare into the face of Jesus and you know—without a doubt—His great love for you. After a time of basking in His love, you stand up, turn around, and are instantly returned home. Now open your eyes.

The goal of this type of exercise is to allow us to use the brain and imagination God gave us for our own good. Sometimes, when we're anxious or fearful, our imagination runs away with scary thoughts and images, so this is a way of using your imagination to bring healing, hope, and peace to your mind. This is imagination therapy!

Another mindfulness technique is to meditate on the Word of God. In the words of Henri Nouwen, meditating on the Word of God means "letting the Word of God descend from our minds into our hearts so that it becomes a part of who we are," so that it "anchors into the center of our being." So that we recognize God's "voice of Love" speaking into the core of our experience.[5]

Psalm 119:15 says, "I meditate on your precepts and consider your ways." Meditating on Scripture, as King David described in the Psalms, simply means that we quiet our minds and souls enough to clearly hear God speaking through His Word (so the seeds can take root and begin to grow). We can also study the character and names or images of God. We can go through guided imagery, as we did in our Sea of Galilee visit, wherein we walk through a scenario that can help bring healing and hope. How might your day be changed after being held in the embrace of a loving Father (*Abba*) or touched by God, your healer (*Jehovah Rapha*)?

In our minds, we can be transported anywhere we want to go. Does the ocean bring peace? Go there right now. Think of the sand between your toes and look out over the crashing waves. Need to be reminded of the peace of God? Imagine the word *peace* floating around all the dark corners of your mind, covering all the upsetting thoughts. As scary as it may sound, it's even mindful to accept negative emotions and just allow yourself to experience them without attempting to explain or resolve them. Instead of avoiding emotions, another mindful approach is to accept the emotions, sit with the fear or the anger or the grief, and don't treat it as a threat.[6] You can use guided imagery or meditation (together or separate) to help you work on reducing stress or dealing with overwhelming life events anytime, anywhere.

Journaling with any or all of these approaches can be helpful. I suggest keeping a journal or a log of the times you use any of these techniques. That way you can refer back and see the outcome, what exercises worked best, and where the breakthrough took place. It may be that you have a recurrent problem. Instead of repeating the same cost-benefit analysis, take another look at the encounter you've already processed. Perhaps you realize that you've been excluding or including costs or benefits that you need to revise.

In this chapter, you've learned about conflict resolution, problem solving, cost-benefit analyses, imagination therapy, and meditating on God's Word. You've also been encouraged to keep all of this together in a journal. Which of these exercises, or combination of exercises, do you resonate with most? What do you plan to use? Start practicing now. Only two chapters remain as we move into the last part of this book: Reclaiming Sanity. Sister, it's time.

PART IV

RECLAIMING SANITY

"Freedom may not come from being in control of life,
but rather from a willingness to move with the events of life."

Rachel Naomi Remen

CHAPTER 17

THROW OUT A LIFELINE: HELPING TRAUMA SURVIVORS

*"Two are better than one, because they have
a good return for their labor."*

Ecclesiastes 4:9

*You may be wondering how to love and support someone who has lived
through a traumatic event. Perhaps you are struggling in this endeavor.
This chapter will offer useful, practical tips for both survivors and their
loved ones while navigating this path together.*

If you're reading this chapter, chances are you're either a hurting
woman who wants support from your loved ones, or you love a hurting woman and want to know how to support her. Whether you're
throwing out a lifeline to those in your life or you're trying to grab
hold of the lifeline for a woman you love, this chapter is for you.

MARY'S STORY

Mary walked toward me with tears in her eyes. I had never met her before, but she hugged me and kissed my cheek anyway. She choked out the words "Thank you" and began to share between sobs how much she appreciated someone acknowledging the ongoing emotional pain she had experienced since the abortion she had some thirty years prior. I had spoken out about this reality at a professional workshop I'd attended, where the speaker had minimized the pain. I didn't know it at the time, but Mary sat in the back row angry and upset until I spoke up.

I didn't know Mary or her story, but I shared what I knew to be true based on what I'd learned while working with clients with similar experiences. Even without being specialized in this area, anyone who sees female clients knows that a number of them will have had abortions. Mary's experience had been written off by therapists in the past, but not this time. I listened carefully as she revealed her story. Mary had bought into the lie that having an abortion should not have had a lasting emotional impact on her, and that her guilt was self-induced or imposed on her by the religious community.

While Mary didn't meet clinical diagnostic criteria for PTSD, she had been traumatized. As a result, she dealt with lingering anxiety and depression. Guilt and shame plagued her, and she believed she had no one to talk with or turn to. The most painful and devastating result was that she believed God had turned His back on her and that she wasn't worthy of love or forgiveness. Mary's entire perspective of herself, others, and the world around her was tainted by her past, and she was searching for comfort and peace. She desperately needed to know that God forgave her the first time she asked, that He loved her fiercely, and that God is who He says He is. She needed a lifeline. So did Peggy.

JOHN AND PEGGY'S STORY

"I don't know how to help her." John sat in my office, frustrated as he shared these words. Peggy sat crying next to him. They had been married only five years, becoming somewhat of a Brady Bunch family that included a mix of children and grandchildren they'd each brought into the relationship.

Because of a complex family situation, one of Peggy's adult children had stopped communicating with her and John, and to add to the injury, they were no longer allowed to see the grandchildren. Peggy's adult daughter, Jenna, had recently revealed some issues from childhood and made it clear there would be no contact for the foreseeable future. As a result, Peggy went through periods when her depression and grief were so severe she would need to be hospitalized.

Ultimately, John couldn't give his wife what she wanted: her child and grandchildren back. Without knowing whether they would ever see the kids again, John was seeking any way possible to support Peggy in her pain. She wanted that too but couldn't quite put her needs into words. John needed help in knowing how to support his hurting wife.

The ripple effect and consequences of sin—both our own and others'—carries long into the future, even after we've repented and sought restoration. The complexity of each perspective and personality involved makes us even more dependent on the grace and mercy God extends to us, so we might also be able to reach toward others. "Serving others is not about forced behavior modification or paying off debts of guilt," said Dr. Rachel Naomi Remen in her book *My Grandfather's Blessings*. "When we serve, we discover that life is holy."

FOUR TIPS

To the woman in a healing process: I encourage you to read through these words, then assess your own needs. Consider sharing this chapter with someone in your life who wants to help you but doesn't know how. Keep in mind that people don't always intuitively know how to help—and they can't read your mind. This chapter will provide some helpful ideas, but ultimately you know yourself and your needs better than anyone, and it's up to you to communicate to those around you what those needs are.

We must learn to speak up for ourselves and express our needs in order to receive what we need. Don't want that pat on the back or the tissue handed to you? Tell your husband. Don't want your friend to give you advice? Ask her to simply listen. (She may even be relieved that you are not looking for her to solve your problems!) The bottom line is we have to help others help us.

To the support person: To those who want to support a woman who has experienced trauma, stress, or an overwhelming life event, thank you for caring about this special woman in your life and for taking the time to learn how to support her. Although therapists aren't supposed to give advice (and I remind my students of this All. The. Time.), I'm going to go ahead and give a little. You see, the best advice I can give you is to learn from that dear woman in your life. I don't have all the answers, but she knows what she needs, even if she can't always put her needs into words easily. Pay careful attention, and you'll start to recognize the cues she gives you for how best to help. She's also being encouraged to work on speaking up for herself and letting you know how you can help. Below are four tips for you to consider together.

1. Let her know you are there for her, but give her space. Allow her to share what and when she wants to share. Don't hover or constantly ask how she's feeling or what she's thinking. When she does open up, be cautious about trying to "fix" things. For example, don't be so quick to hand her a tissue or pat her back, telling her things will be okay. The reality is that you cannot fix her or her problems, so don't bother trying. It won't work.

Speaking of tissues, the great tissue debate comes up every time I teach a counseling course wherein we discuss what to do when a client starts crying. The question becomes: "To hand a tissue, or not to hand a tissue?" It's always a funny experience to sit with a room full of future counselors debating this issue. And let me tell you, folks can get passionate about this topic! Some women make it clear they always want to be handed a tissue so as not to mess up their makeup or have snot running down their face, while others are adamant that when they are handed a tissue, the message they receive is "Stop crying!" Sometimes they get the impression that the person handing them a tissue can't handle what they're sharing, or even their tears. Through trial and error, you can learn what your loved one wants. Just ask her. She'll tell you whether she wants a tissue handed to her. With this and all communication, be as compassionate and sensitive as possible.

Ultimately, it's so important that you are willing to simply sit with her as she shares what's on her heart. Through our sessions, it became apparent there were times when Peggy wanted to spend time alone to cry and grieve, while at other times she wanted John to comfort her. Since John couldn't read her mind, it was up to Peggy to tell her husband clearly what her needs were, and then it was up to him to respect her wishes.

If you are reading this chapter in order to better assist an overwhelmed or stressed-out woman, please understand things may not always be equal in the support department. And, ladies, if on your healing journey you encounter someone in your care network who has also suffered trauma, my encouragement is to remember the Golden Rule: Treat others the way you want to be treated, as the words of Matthew 7:12 instruct us. You cannot always receive support without being willing to provide support. There will be times when you have more needs, and times when the other person has more. While everyone deserves support, not everyone is capable of giving it.

2. Be patient and flexible. In 1 Corinthians 13:4, we're told that love is patient. In working with dozens of individuals diagnosed with PTSD and other disorders, I learned very quickly that it can take *a lot* of patience and flexibility to be in a relationship (family, friendship, or romantic) with someone who has experienced trauma. Trauma affects one's ability to be intimate (emotionally and physically). Additionally, the way life is lived changes after trauma. What used to be everyday, routine (even fun) errands and events become a challenge. I know many people who need to leave a store or event as soon as they arrive. They don't plan to need to leave so quickly, but they may experience a trigger and become anxious or panicked. While we don't want to encourage people to avoid, we do want to respect the boundaries and current condition and capabilities of our loved ones. The saying "Meet them where they are" comes to mind. Hopefully, her work toward recovery continues, but wherever she is currently is wherever she is currently. This has to be respected and honored.

One suggestion is to drive to events in separate cars so that you can each leave when you're ready. You could also work up to events slowly. For example, if she is fearful of going to a movie theater, try to re-create the movie theater feel at home first. Several "rehearsals" may be needed to move closer and closer before she is ready to go to the movies. And if she's never ready, your acceptance that she is not comfortable with this is the most helpful response. Maybe you knew her before she experienced trauma and you hope to help her "get back to being her old self." Understand that she may never be the same, but that doesn't mean she and your relationship can't thrive.

3. Encourage her to seek mental health treatment if needed, and participate with her. Throughout this book, I have mentioned mental health treatment. While not everyone who has experienced a negative life event needs this type of intervention, if your loved one is suffering with negative thoughts, feelings, or behaviors that are problematic for her or your relationship, she may need some encouragement to seek professional help. Be very careful here. You don't want to imply that she is "crazy." If you have any questions about that, reread chapter 1!

The reality is that she is *not* going crazy but rather having a reaction to an abnormal event. If the resulting issues don't resolve on their own, she may benefit from treatment specifically designed to help with these types of problems. And you know what? You might benefit from going as well—learning more from a professional about how you can best help and encourage your loved one, in particular if you are a family member living in the same home. It's also important to recognize that you also may be affected negatively as a result of your loved one's trauma. There are various terms to describe this phenomenon, but here we will use *secondary trauma*. While this is not a diagnosis found in the *Diagnostic and Statistical Manual of Mental Disorders*, secondary trauma is faced by many who are very involved in the life of someone who has experienced trauma firsthand. The symptoms can mimic those of PTSD and should be taken seriously. If you are experiencing any symptoms described earlier in this book, please consider the benefit of getting professional help for yourself. You cannot be there to support or help anyone else effectively if you are not taking good care of yourself.

John and Peggy knew they both needed professional treatment, so it was not a difficult decision for them to make. Once there, they realized the need for both marital counseling and individual counseling. The reality is that there are no guarantees that mental health treatment will fully resolve a problem someone is facing; however, it can certainly provide healthy coping skills, tools, and resources for helping your loved one to address and manage her symptoms, as well as your own.

4. Nurture your faith together. There is great power in believers coming together to pray and ask for God's guidance together. Matthew 18:20 says, "Where two or three gather in my name, there am I with them." Worship together, pray together, read Scripture together. A dear friend and I were going through similar circumstances related to career change. We committed to pray together over the phone every week until these issues were resolved. After those issues were resolved, other issues came up. We realized that there would always be stressors in life and that we benefit greatly from spending time in prayer together.

It is impossible for one chapter to cover all you need to know in order to help your loved one, but this is a start. Your loved one needs compassion. She needs a listening ear. She needs you. And as you help care for her emotional needs, don't forget to care for your own needs as well. Self-care is important for us all. You cannot give what you don't have. Think of yourself as a water well and your support for your loved one as water. If you keep giving until the well is dry, you will have nothing else to give. May your own well be filled so your loved one is blessed from the overflow. In his book *Why, O Lord?* Carlo Carretto warns us that "love will make demands on us. It will question us from within. It will disturb us. Sadden us. Play havoc with our feelings. Harass us. Reveal our superficialities. But at last it will bring us to the light."[1] And in that light we will be free.

CHAPTER 18

REIMAGINE: A MINI RETREAT

"Jesus looked at them and said, 'With man this is impossible, but with God all things are possible.'"

Matthew 19:26

*In this final chapter, I suggest taking a mini retreat in order to relax and better manage stressors and emotions. Here, we'll apply some practical activities and work through helpful exercises that help you do just that. The best part is that we'll take time to go deeper with the Lord in Scripture. There's also a quick journey back through the four parts of this book, with small actionable steps toward **reclaiming sanity**.*

Remember how I said I'd love for us to be together sipping tea and eating something delicious? It's true, I want us to be together. Since we're not in my living room, imagine we're at a spa together. All those pesky electronics are turned off, your kids and husband are set for the next few hours, and we've slipped into lush robes and are reclining on loungers. The aroma of this place is like fresh air after a spring rain—clean and light. The music is gentle; the lighting is soft and perfect. Of course chocolate is right at our fingertips. What you need is a little quiet, a little TLC; a safe space to sit with the idea of saneness, stability, sound wisdom.

You or your loved ones may have survived a great and terrible loss (maybe you are still in the midst of overwhelming and stressful situations), but survival is not a lifestyle to settle into. You want to participate in God's creative, redemptive work and continue healing and growing. You have an idea of what that looks like, but life keeps rolling or crashing in at such a crazy pace, you don't have time to sit with this new picture of what you want for your life. I suggest a little retreat like the one you just imagined. If that's not possible, how about a mini retreat?

Instead of massages and mud baths (but why not—those can be included), you and your most trusted friend can do a mini retreat to try new techniques for relaxing, unwinding, untangling, massaging out that knot in the back of your neck, your shoulders, the pressure in your head, or in your gut. The best part is a beautiful toolbox of resources I have gathered together for you. Acquaint yourself with them here, so after you return to your daily routine, you can pull out any one of the tools in the moment you need it most. These tools don't take up space, never wear out, and get better with use, like that worn-in sweatshirt you'll never get rid of no matter what it looks like.

You want to manage your emotions and improve your well-being—for the long haul. In this mini retreat, we're going to brainstorm quick tips, not only for managing emotions but also for healing in body, soul, spirit, and relationships. I will walk you through managing potential stressors, taking a personal time-out, retraining the cleansing practice of breathing, and learning how to relax your body. This isn't your typical retreat, but you can set aside your life for whatever margin of time you do have to focus on taking care of yourself. We'll rest, remember, reimagine, and restore.

For just a little while, you will give yourself permission to step away and forget about your never-ending mundane tasks (laundry, dishes, yard work). You will set aside the nagging voices that put you down and say you'll never get it all together. You won't fret about the kids or the hubby or work or anything else that you invest so much of your life in. This is y-o-u time. Doctor's orders. Yes, I'm "prescribing" this. Why? I need my mini retreat and a stocked toolbox as much as you do!

On this retreat, we offer a variety of amazing choices, depending on how much time you have.

> *Option #1: Calming Breaths – 15 minutes*
> *Option #2: Progressive Muscle Relaxation – 30 minutes*
> *Option #3: Personal Time-Out – 60 minutes*
> *Option #4: Reclaiming Sanity Retreat – 2 hours*

You don't have to follow these in order. You can choose one option now and come back later for another. Or you can work straight through and do them all. Regardless, you can engage in portions of this mini retreat or the entire mini retreat again and again. Now, it's time to prepare for your escape into the lap of emotional luxury.

PREPARE FOR YOUR RETREAT

All you need for your retreat is this book, a Bible, and a quiet place by yourself or with a few of your girlfriends who are in as much need of this retreat as you are. You might also want to have some cool water, light snacks, quiet music, and some comfy walking shoes in case you want to take a relaxed stroll as you pray or meditate. Perhaps you want to take a journal or sketchbook and pencils with you.

Before we dive into any of the available mini-retreat options, it will help you fully engage if you manage potential stressors that might interfere with your ability to focus and get the most out of your time here. We know stress is inevitable and unavoidable. We've already talked about the difference between eustress and distress. Regardless of which kind you may be experiencing, as a result of stress, you are more likely to experience troublesome thoughts, negative emotions, and problematic behaviors. You need to take care of yourself in order to manage your stress level. I know that's why you're here, and I want this to be as powerful as possible. So take a moment and write down everything that is heavy on your heart and mind. While some of it may come up as we work through activities, commit to staying in this moment. Stay present, in the here and now. Unless you are addressing one of these issues in a healthy manner as outlined in these pages, set these bothers aside, at least for now. Go ahead and write down what's weighing you down:

_____

_____

_____

This is a good technique for getting things off your mind in order to sleep more soundly too. Now, move ahead to whatever option you have chosen to get you started on your mini retreat.

Option #1: Calming Breaths

We are reminded throughout the Bible (such as in Matthew 6) to be anxious about nothing. But this is much easier said than done. The calming-breath exercise helps you relax when you are feeling worried or angry—when you feel jittery and as though you just can't calm down. This is a simple three-step process for controlling your breathing. It's different from just deep breathing. This will help reduce the physical and emotional symptoms you are experiencing. You've allotted fifteen minutes for this activity, but you can take as much or as little time as you need. You can even combine this with other activities such as imagination therapy. Here's how it works:

  1. Take a deep breath through your nose and hold your breath to the count of three.

2. Slowly let the breath out through your mouth while thinking of a calming word such as *relax* or *peace*.

3. Repeat until you feel calm.

Option #2: Progressive Muscle Relaxation

This is another activity that will help you calm down.[1] Practice it by sitting in a quiet room with your eyes closed and your feet flat on the ground. For each part of the body mentioned below, you should tense your muscles for about ten seconds before relaxing completely. In time, you will be able to tense and release during times of stress, anger, or anxiety. It's also helpful for those who have trouble sleeping. In order to make this a habit, you must practice regularly. So tense tight and relax completely. Just let go and see how relaxed you feel afterward.

Right hand and forearm: clench your right fist.

Right upper arm: bend your right arm at the elbow and flex.

Left hand and forearm: clench your left fist.

Left upper arm: bend your left arm at the elbow and flex.

Forehead: raise your eyebrows as high as they will go.

Middle portion of your face: wrinkle your nose.

Lower face: press your lips and teeth together.

Upper back: pull your shoulders back as far as they will go.

Chest and abdomen: pull your shoulders forward and tense your stomach.

Right upper leg: raise your right leg an inch off the ground and make it rigid.

Right calf: point your right foot and toes forward.

Right ankle: point your foot and toes upward.

Left upper leg: raise your left leg an inch off the ground and make it rigid.

Left calf: point your left foot and toes forward.

Left ankle: point your foot and toes upward.

Are you relaxed yet? You may have spent so long feeling tense that relaxing seems impossible to you. Keep practicing progressive muscle relaxation and you'll find yourself starting to relax. We all need a break from the real world. Time to sink into that robe, tune out social media, and relax. When we take opportunities to relax and destress, we can handle real life better, and we're more prepared to manage upsetting thoughts and feelings as soon as we notice them cropping up. Anytime you need a break, go back through this option. The spa is never closed.

Option #3: Personal Time-Out

We are called to rest (Mark 6:31). In Matthew 11:28, Jesus tells us to come to Him when we are weary and heavy laden and He will give us rest. While rest is important for the Sabbath (after all, God rested on the seventh day of creation, before the fall, which tells us it was a part of His original plan), rest is critical at other times in our lives. It's not about being unproductive. It's about taking time to ensure we can be our very best, giving our bodies and minds a break from the daily grind of life. Rest isn't just for physical restoration; it's for emotional restoration as well, especially during times of conflict.

Coaches call time-outs during athletic events for players to cool down and regroup before getting back in the game. You can do this too! A personal time-out (PTO), is a period of time you can take to calm down, clear your mind, and then return to resolve the problem. Just like sports, right? In order for a PTO to be successful, it's imperative that you talk to your loved ones about your PTO plan before deciding to implement it. They need to know that you are going to utilize this tool. It is equally important for you to allow your loved ones to use personal time-outs too, if they wish. Here are the steps to taking a personal time-out:

1. Recognize early warning signs of negative emotions or reactions.

2. Tell your loved one you need to step away for a period of time to calm down.

3. Assure the loved one you will return to work on your problem after you calm down.

4. If your loved one responds negatively, remind him or her that you are trying to regain control of yourself so you can deal more reasonably.

5. Spend at least an hour away. This time should be used for calming down. Perhaps use the calming-breaths exercise or progressive muscle relaxation. You can journal, read Scripture, draw, or pray.

Take a walk, go through a cost-benefit analysis, or practice the four steps of assertiveness. Perhaps take a nap or watch something lighthearted to help ease your mood. No matter what you do during this time, use it to help regain control over your negative thoughts and feelings.

6. Once you are calm, and the other person is as well, return to address the issue. Or perhaps what is needed is for you to apologize and get back on the right track with your loved one.

Anytime you start to feel stressed out or overwhelmed, call a personal time-out. If you've got children, they'll understand the concept, although they may not understand why anyone would *want* or *choose* to take a time-out. For an adult it's not punishment, but it is a discipline. You are working on the disciplines of being patient, being in control of your reactions, and managing your emotions. One time, I called a personal time-out when I found myself getting heated in a discussion with my boss. He was a little surprised, but very receptive. (He was, after all, a psychiatrist.) If you're going to use this technique with a coworker or your employer, you might want to run it past them first, but a simple "I think it may be helpful if I take some time to think about this before continuing this conversation. Would that be okay?" may suffice. It may or may not work, but it's worth a shot. As with all the exercises and activities in this mini retreat, you have to try them out (more than once) to know if they work for you.

Option #4: Reclaiming Sanity Retreat

Ecclesiastes 3:1–8 tells us there is a time for everything:

There is a time for everything,
and a season for every activity under the
heavens:

a time to be born and a time to die,
a time to plant and a time to uproot,
a time to kill and a time to heal,
a time to tear down and a time to build,
a time to weep and a time to laugh,
a time to mourn and a time to dance,
a time to scatter stones and a time to gather
them,
a time to embrace and a time to refrain from
embracing,
a time to search and a time to give up,
a time to keep and a time to throw away,
a time to tear and a time to mend,
a time to be silent and a time to speak,
a time to love and a time to hate,
a time for war and a time for peace.

The reclaiming sanity retreat option gives you the opportunity to go back through this book, review some highlights, and apply some content presented earlier. It is a reminder that there is time for everything, including time to cry, time to forgive, and time (so much time!) to pray.

PART I. RECLAIMING CLARITY (30 MINUTES)

1. A Time to Be Kind

Remember that trauma and loss bring a whole mix of emotion. Befriend yours. Attend to your soul with gentle kindness. Don't let it run roughshod over you. Instead, develop a habit where you promise you'll attend to it as you would a small child who is upset and frightened. Treat yourself with love, respect, kindness, and forgiveness. If you are experiencing shame (such as telling yourself "I am bad") instead of guilt (such as telling yourself "I did something bad"), I encourage you to seek additional help. There are many solid resources available if you want to work on this yourself, but this is also a great reason to seek counseling. When you feel good, allow yourself the freedom to experience this without self-sabotage or condemnation. Give yourself time to heal. In an era of instant-everything, this is hard to accept. Give yourself grace and patience like a sweet aunt would. Life is hard; we need to be kind—even to ourselves.

2. A Time to Reclaim Christ's Companionship in Suffering

a. Time to Name. Chapter 3 discusses turning triggers into monuments of God's faithful love. Write out what monuments you will

create to honor God instead of honing in on the negative reminders that places, people, sights, or sounds conjure up.

_____

_____

_____

_____

_____

b. Time to Pray. Praying the names of God is a helpful way to
remember the many characteristics of God. As you read the lists
below, call God by each name, thanking Him for specific ways He
has revealed that part of Himself to you. Also, spend time pouring
out your heart's deepest desire for God to show up in a big way in
any of these areas that you are in need of.

> Elohay Mishpat – God of Justice
> Elohay Selichot – God of Forgiveness
> Elohay Mikarov – God Who Is Near
> Elohay Mauzi – God of My Strength
> Elohay Tehilati – God of My Praise
> Elohay Yishi – God of My Salvation
> Immanuel – God Is with Us
> Jehovah M'kadesh – The Lord Who
> Makes Holy
> Jehovah Yireh – The Lord Who Sees
> and Provides
> Jehovah Shalom – The Lord of Peace
> Jehovah Rapha – The Lord Who Heals

c. Time to Cry. John 11:35 is the shortest verse in the Bible: "Jesus wept." It's not surprising that Jesus cried, since He was human. What may give us pause is why He cried. Jesus cried because His friend Lazarus had died, and because Lazarus's sisters, Mary and Martha, were deeply saddened. Although Jesus knew He was going to bring Lazarus back to life, He still shed tears over one friend dying and other friends grieving, as anyone would. The salty, watery release of tears is included in our physiological design to be a cleansing release. Crying is a gift and can be a prayer of relinquishment. Here, you are being given permission to cry. Feel free to shed these tears, which are guaranteed to provide you an emotional release.

PART II. RECLAIMING ME (30 MINUTES)

3. A Time to Remove Masks

Chapter 8 highlighted anger as being a mask for other emotions, but women tend to wear masks to cover depression, fears, marital problems, problems with children, and more. For this mini retreat to be helpful, these masks need to be removed. You might find it helpful to literally wash your face as a symbol of removing the masks. Commit to being who you really are, rather than a character. Every day is not Halloween, and you cannot escape who you are by covering up. More on who you really are next.

4. A Time to Know My True Identity in Christ

The journey to reclaiming your truest redeemed self looks a lot like hiking the Pacific Rim Trail. It will have a lot of ups and downs and narrow trails—even some hairpin curves. As your healing progresses, you'll find your thoughts are clearer, your judgments are more sound and reliable, your concentration is improved, you have a desire to be with others and to do more for others, you are stronger, and you are more content. But you have to know who you really are in order to get there. You have to know your true identity in Christ. Below, write out who you and others say you are, and then compare that to who God says you are. Use the Scripture to back up these statements. Write out some of these truths on sticky notes, and tack them in strategic places around your home, office, or even your car so you can see them on a regular basis.

Who I or others say I am   *versus*   *Who God says I am*

_____   _____

_____   _____

_____   _____

PART III. RECLAIMING PEACE (30 MINUTES)

5. A Time to Forgive and Rebuild

Now that forgiveness and rebuilding relationships have been covered, how do you plan to apply these principles to your life? Below, or in your journal, write out the names of those you need to forgive and those you need to restore relationships with, along with a plan for making this happen. Don't forget about yourself— not only might you need to forgive yourself, but it's very likely you need to reconcile with yourself as well.

_____

_____

_____

_____

After you have completed that challenging task, spend some time in prayer asking the Lord to help you daily to commit to forgive and restore where possible.

6. A Time to Be Mindful

Now that you have the idea behind mindfulness, let's walk through one more mindful exercise. Sit back and relax. But only for a moment before you are transported into a bustling snowstorm in the middle of a field. Although you were barely inching your car forward on the highway, only able to barely see the taillights of the car in the front of you, you slid off the road and deep into a field. You can't tell what kind of field because of the snow that is blowing all around you. After spinning around in several circles, you come to a dead stop. You pause for a moment, startled, before thinking through what to do next.

Once you realize you are okay and your car is still in one piece, you shiver and pull your coat a bit tighter before attempting to start your car. You turn the key, but nothing happens. You try again. Same result. The car will not start and you become afraid. You panic as you realize you have no cell phone service. Until you start to hear a voice, faint at first, but getting louder. "Are you okay?" the deep male voice calls out.

You muster up the loudest outdoor voice you can and yell back, "Yes, but my car won't start." Moments later you hear, "Follow my voice." You realize there is someone, somewhere, who is trying to help you find your way out of the blizzard mess. In that moment, you know you have two choices: follow the stranger or stay stuck in the car with no heat and no phone service. You decide to take a chance, so you quickly grab your purse and head out into the field of snow, following the man's voice until you reach him at the road. Once you make it there, you realize it's a trucker who happened to be driving behind you and saw you veer off the road. He has already radioed in for paramedics and police, and they are on the way. You breathe a huge sigh of relief as you get in the warm cab of his truck to wait.

Although not totally relaxing, this guided imagery takes you through the process of deciding when to trust by faith. This is what Jesus asks you to do. He is calling out to you, "Follow My voice," and you have to decide whether you are going to follow Him.

PART IV. RECLAIMING SANITY (30 MINUTES)

7. A Time to Act

When you are stressed or suffering, it's easy to get overwhelmed with seemingly simple tasks or even day-to-day life. Set a basic schedule that doesn't require too many decisions, and stick to it. When your inner world is chaotic, a light schedule helps anchor you to a frame of sanity. Keep in mind that Sundays can be the hardest day of the week if you don't surround yourself in worship and a small community of believers. Saturdays can be tough too; schedule comforting activities for the weekend.

Have trouble remembering what you need to do or when? Tailor-make your own to-do list and stick it on the fridge. Better yet, put the tasks on your calendar! Dr. John Grat provides a list of one hundred oxytocin-producing activities for a woman to engage in—which lower stress! You'll find a baker's dozen of his ideas below to stimulate your own ideas:

- Get a massage
- Get a manicure or pedicure
- Phone time with a friend
- Listen to favorite music
- Paint a picture with a friend
- Donate gently used clothes to charity
- Take a scented bath by candlelight
- Cook together with a loved one
- Care for others with a home-cooked meal
- Attend a play
- Spend time at the river, beach, or lake
- Keep a photo journal
- Volunteer at a local hospital

Bonus: A word on holidays, since they can be especially difficult for those who have experienced trauma. One helpful tip is to plan ahead so that the holidays are not right on top of you. Many people don't have energy to give gifts or to be with family, or they don't have family or traditions. Don't let yourself go down the dark hole of negative thoughts and feelings about all of this. And don't avoid the holidays or allow them to sneak up on you. Plan to be with friends who are low maintenance and fun!

8. A Time to Celebrate

Do an audit of all the good things in your life worth celebrating. As the saying goes, count your blessings; name them one by one. Write them all down in your journal, and read them frequently. Spend time thanking God for all you have. Rejoice over the smallest of victories. Enjoy life, and be thankful for it, keeping in mind that life is only a vapor.[2]

CLOSING THOUGHTS

I walked into the office for the mobile gymnastics company I worked for one day in early summer 2000. The director, Cari, was playing a song I'd never heard before. The words were almost haunting, and I asked her about the song. She explained it was a song by Ginny Owens titled "If You Want Me To." I instantly felt a connection with this song and went out and bought the tape (yes, *tape*). I listened to the song over and over again as I drove my mama's old station wagon from one preschool to the next to teach the kids how to walk on a balance beam and jump on a trampoline. The words that would not leave my mind are as follows:

The pathway is broken and the signs are unclear
And I don't know the reason why You brought
                    me here
But just because You love me the way that You do
I'm gonna walk through the valley if You want me to
'Cause I'm not who I was when I took my first step
And I'm clinging to the promise You're not through
                    with me yet
So if all of these trials bring me closer to You
Then I will go through the fire if You want me to
It may not be the way I would have chosen
When You lead me through a world that's not
                    my home
But You never said it would be easy
You only said I'd never go alone
So when the whole world turns against me and
                    I'm all by myself
And I can't hear You answer my cries for help
I'll remember the suffering Your love put You
                    through
And I will go through the valley if You want me to

I sit in a coffee shop with tears stinging my eyes as I type these last few words and listen to this song once again. You see, I heard that song for the first time a few weeks before I had my lifesaving surgery. God was preparing me for what would be the most challenging time in my life. Many years later, as I sat in a church service, this song began to play over the sound system. Completely emotionally unprepared, I burst into tears. The flurry of feelings was mostly related to the fact that, although I walked through a valley, God was with me the whole way. He never left me or abandoned me. Oh, sister, He has never left or abandoned you either. I hate that suffering plagues this world, but thank God this is not our home!

The night before my surgery, Cari called me. She offered to pray with me before I went in for the operation, and she wanted to make sure I was saved, that I had asked Jesus Christ to forgive me of my sins and made Him Lord of my life. I can't end this book without asking you the same. If you've never taken this step and you would like to, it's so simple—and completely life changing. If you are ready, you can say this prayer:

> "Dear Lord, please forgive me of my sins. Thank You for dying on the cross and paying the penalty for my sins so that I don't have to suffer the consequences for eternity. Thank You for loving me. I want You to be the Lord of my life. In the name of Jesus, amen."

I'm praying for you. That you'll experience relief from your trauma, stress, or overwhelming life events. And you know what? I know without a doubt you will experience complete relief when you meet Jesus. Until then, there will always be triggers, stressors, events that tip the scales. We have a known path to walk. Our job is to choose and claim again the choice we made the day before. We will choose again tomorrow.

You've gotten some answers.

You have begun healing.

You are still alive.

You are so loved.

You are already healing.

You are *not* crazy.

You are reclaiming sanity.

HELPFUL RESOURCES

The Cry of the Soul: How Our Emotions Reveal Our Deepest Questions about God by Dan B. Allender and Tremper Longman III

Lord I Want to Know You by Kay Arthur

Life Together by Dietrich Bonhoeffer

Extraordinary Women by Julie Clinton

Turn Your Life Around by Tim Clinton

Boundaries: When to Say Yes, How to Say No to Take Control of Your Life by Henry Cloud and John Townsend

When God Weeps: Why Our Sufferings Matter to the Almighty by Joni Eareckson Tada and Steven Estes

Let. It. Go.: How to Stop Running the Show and Start Walking in Faith by Karen Ehman

Kingdom Woman: Embracing Your Purpose, Power, and Possibilities by Tony Evans and Chrystal Evans Hurst

Rest Assured by Bill Ewing

You're Going to Be Okay: Encouraging Truth Your Heart Needs to Hear, Especially on the Hard Days by Holley Gerth

Addiction and Grace by Archibald D. Hart

Adrenaline and Stress by Archibald D. Hart

Living Forward by Michael Hyatt and Daniel Harkavy

Embrace Grace by Liz Curtis Higgs

Giddy Up, Eunice (Because Women Need Each Other) by Sophie Hudson

Could It Be This Simple? A Biblical Model for Healing the Mind by Timothy R. Jennings

A Grief Observed by C. S. Lewis

The Dark Night of the Soul by Gerald G. May

So Long Insecurity, You've Been a Bad Friend to Us by Beth Moore

Fervent: A Woman's Battle Plan for Serious, Specific, and Strategic Prayer by Priscilla Shirer

The DNA of Relationships by Gary Smalley

Forgive and Forget by Lewis B. Smedes

Shame and Grace by Lewis B. Smedes

Praying the Names of God: A Daily Guide by Ann Spangler (also, *Praying the Names of Jesus*)

Unglued: Making Wise Decisions in the Midst of Raw Emotions by Lysa TerKeurst

The PTSD Workbook by Marybeth Williams and Soili Poijula

Hope Heals: A True Story of Overwhelming Loss and an Overcoming Love by Katherine and Jay Wolf

Whole: An Honest Look at the Holes in Your Life --And How to Let God Fill Them by Lisa Whittle

BONUS: ANGER CUES AND ANGER SCALE

A simple way to monitor anger is to use a 1 to 10 scale.[1] A score of 1 on the anger scale represents a complete lack of anger or a total state of calm, and a score of 10 represents an angry and explosive loss of control. The higher your anger score is, the more you experience negative physical, emotional, behavioral, and cognitive cues to anger.

Physical cues include:
- rapid heartbeat
- nausea
- tightness in chest
- tension headaches
- feeling hot

Behavioral clues include:
- pacing
- clenching fists
- raising voice
- staring

Emotional cues include:
- feeling fear
- feeling hurt
- feeling jealous
- feeling guilty

Cognitive cues include:
- negative self-talk
- images of aggression
- contemplating revenge

The goal here is to notice when any of these cues are present and to practice your tools to calm you down *before* your anger gets out of control.

BONUS: DEALING WITH ROAD RAGE

Can you recall a time when *you* got angry while driving? Of course you can; every driver can to differing degrees. If you have found yourself far too close to putting yourself or others in danger while driving angry or exploding into rage at other drivers, this exercise is for you.

Thinking back on a road rage incident, how you do feel now? Was it really necessary? Do you think there is anything you could have done to avoid the anger? Why did you get *so* angry?

You may recall that according to the Road Rage Driver Stress Profile,[2] four potential problem areas are identified for drivers:

- anger
- impatience
- competitiveness
- punitiveness

If any of these come up for you when in traffic, practice your calm-breathing exercise while driving. When tempted to become angry, ask yourself, "What is the cost of this anger versus the benefit of this anger?" Use your tools!

One of the best techniques to avoid road rage is to drive defensively. Below are some tips to stay safe and prevent road rage, but I encourage you to consider taking a defensive driving class. It was "requested" that I take this class, and despite my resistance, I learned a lot!

TIPS TO STAY SAFE AND PREVENT ROAD RAGE

1. Leave early so you're not concerned about being late. When you are concerned about being late, your irritability level can quickly turn into anger and your driving may become unsafe.

2. Place Post-It notes in your car that provide calming thoughts such as: "I need to think before I act" or "I will be off the road soon."

3. Listen to relaxing music. Be careful not to listen to music that increases your heart rate.

4. Use stress balls during stop-and-go traffic.

5. Don't tailgate! Leave enough room between your car and the car in front of you.

6. Use your horn sparingly. It is appropriate to use a horn in certain circumstances, but overuse may increase your road rage—or someone else's.

7. Don't make eye contact with angry drivers.

8. Slow down! As the saying goes, "Better late than dead."

9. Pay attention 100 percent of the time.

10. Put on turn signals. Always. And don't rely on others to use theirs.

11. Be careful about distractions. This means: do not eat, text, or put on makeup while driving. If you must use your phone, consider using an earpiece.

12. Move to the right. Slower traffic should always stay to the right—and you should be among the slower traffic.

13. Check intersections when the light is green to ensure all cross traffic is stopped.

14. Be careful about blind spots. Always look before you change lanes.

15. Stop at yellow lights. Better safe than sorry!

16. Pray before you begin to travel. Pray frequently while you are driving. And remember to thank God for protecting you once you arrive safely at your destination.

ACKNOWLEDGMENTS

A heartfelt thank-you to David C Cook publishers and Alice Crider for dreaming about and developing this book with me.

To my agent, Diana Flegal, with Hartline Literary Agency: Thank you for taking a chance on me. I'm so grateful for your kindness, encouragement, and wisdom.

To Dr. Donna K. Wallace: You helped ease the load in bringing this book to life. It's far more powerful than it would have been without you. When I think of you, I think of Ecclesiastes 4:9, "Two are better than one, because they have a good return for their labor." Thank you!

My life has been richly blessed through many friends. It would be impossible to list anyone individually for fear I would forget someone—and that would keep me awake at night. So, you know who you are, sweet friends. Thank you for your love and support.

To my dear family, I love you all and pray for you daily. Mama and Daddy, it's hard to put into words how much you mean to me. Hopefully you just know. Bubba and Big Red, being your aunt is my honor and one of the greatest privileges of my life. To my siblings, in-laws, aunts, uncles, and cousins, I love being a part of this wonderful family!

Nick, meeting you on February 23, 2001, changed the course of my life. You told me that day you would marry me—not only did you make good on that promise, but you've made good on your wedding vows each and every day of our marriage. As the words of Philippians 1:3 say, "I thank my God every time I remember you."

To my Lord and Savior Jesus Christ, thank You for Your grace and mercy. I pray the words of this book, and their impact, bring glory to our Father.

ABOUT THE AUTHOR

Dr. Laurel Shaler holds a PhD in counselor education and supervision, and is a licensed social worker, national certified counselor, and former psychotherapist for the Department of Veterans Affairs. She is a department chair at Liberty University in the Department of Counselor Education and Family Studies. Laurel also speaks and writes on the intersections of faith, culture, and emotional well-being.

As a part of the Thomas Road Baptist Church women's ministry, Laurel was a regular contributor for the *Coffee Break* daily devotionals, which are distributed to 15,000+ women daily. She has also been a contributor to the *American Association of Christian Counselors* blog, the *Bound for Life* blog, the *To Save a Life* and *For Every Mom* blogs, and the *Southern Baptist Convention's Ethics and Religious Liberty Commission* blog. Laurel is a She Speaks graduate, has been a contributor for www.believe.com, and has been published by Lifeway's *Journey Magazine, Extraordinary Women, P31 Woman*, and *Just Between Us*.

Laurel posts regularly on her website and blog, found at www.drlaurelshaler.com. You can connect with her on Facebook at www.facebook.com/drlaurelshaler or Twitter (@DrLaurelShaler). She has been married to Nicholas "Nick" Shaler, a naval officer, since 2003. They live in Greenville, South Carolina, and are in the process of adopting. Laurel's loves include her family (especially her two nephews) and anything sweet.

NOTES

CHAPTER 1: AM I GOING CRAZY?

1. Retrieved from www.ptsd.va.gov.

2. Merriam-Webster, s.v. "trauma," www.merriam-webster.com/dictionary/trauma.

3. Merriam-Webster, s.v. "stress," www.merriam-webster.com/dictionary/stress.

4. "Eustress vs. Distress," Brock University, accessed March 28, 2017, www.brocku.ca/health-services/health-education/stress/eustress-distress.

CHAPTER 2: THE FOURTEEN-POUND ...

1. F. J. Raabe and D. Spengler, "Epigenetic Risk Factors in PTSD and Depression," *Frontiers in Psychiatry*, 2013, 1.

CHAPTER 3: YOU'RE NOT ALONE

1. Psalm 46:7.

CHAPTER 4: UNDERSTANDING POST-TRAUMATIC STRESS DISORDER (PTSD)

1. American Psychological Association, *Diagnostic and Statistical Manual of Mental Disorders*, 5th ed., 2011.

2. F. Naeem et al., "Prevalence and Psychosocial Risk Factors of PTSD," *Journal of Affective Disorders*, 2011; C. Xue, et al., "A Meta-Analysis of Risk Factors for Combat-Related PTSD among Military Personnel and Veterans," *PloS One*, 2015.

3. M. C. Goslin et al., "Identifying Youth at Risk for Difficulties Following a Traumatic Event: Pre-event Factors Are Associated with Acute Symptomatology," *Journal of Traumatic Stress*, 2013.

4. F. J. Raabe and D. Spengler, "Epigenic Risk Factors in PTSD and Depression," *Frontiers in Psychiatry*, 2013, 1.

5. A. T. Moller et al., "Identifying Risk Factors for PTSD in Women Seeking Medical Help After Rape," *Plos One*, 2014.

6. F. Naeem, et al., "Prevalence and Psychosocial Risk Factors of PTSD," *Journal of Affective Disorders*, 2011.

7. C. Xue, et al., "A Meta-Analysis of Risk Factors for Combat-Related PTSD among Military Personnel and Veterans," *PloS One*, 2015.

8. National Center for PTSD, www.ptsd.va.gov.

9. I. Jarero and L. Artigas, "The EMDR Integrative Group Treatment Protocol: EMDR Group Treatment for Early Intervention Following Critical Incidents," *European Review of Applied Psychology*, 2010.

10. J. C. Ipser and D. J. Stein, "Evidence-Based Pharmacotherapy of Post-traumatic Stress Disorder (PTSD)," *International Journal of Neuropsychopharmacology*, 2011.

CHAPTER 6: MORE THAN A BAND-AID: HOPE AND HEALING START HERE

1. Matt Maher, "Lord, I Need You."

2. Found at InwardOutward.org.

CHAPTER 7: DEALING WITH A TOUGH PAST

1. Susan Krauss Whitbourne, "The Essential Guide to Defense Mechanisms," *Psychology Today*, October 22, 2011, www.psychologytoday.com/blog /fulfillment-any-age/201110/the-essential-guide-defense-mechanisms.

2. Patrick M. Reilly and Michael S. Shopshire, *Anger Management for Substance Abuse and Mental Health Clients: A Cognitive Behavioral Therapy Manual*, Substance Abuse and Mental Health Services Administration, US Department of Health and Human Services, 2002, 11, http://store.samhsa.gov/shin/content//SMA13-4213/SMA13-4213.pdf.

3. Dan B. Allender and Tremper Longman III, *The Cry of the Soul: How Our Emotions Reveal Our Deepest Questions about God* (Colorado Springs: NavPress, 1994), 258.

CHAPTER 8: FACES OF FRUSTRATION

1. Melba Colgrove, Harold Bloomfield, and Peter McWilliams, *How to Survive the Loss of a Love* (Los Angeles: Prelude Press, 1991), 94.

2. Dan B. Allender and Tremper Longman, III, *Cry of the Soul: How Our Emotions Reveal Our Deepest Questions about God* (Colorado Springs: NavPress, 1994), back cover.

3. Allender and Longman, *Cry of the Soul*, back cover.

4. Patrick M. Reilly and Michael S. Shopshire, *Anger Management for Substance Abuse and Mental Health Clients: A Cognitive Behavioral Therapy Manual*, Substance Abuse and Mental Health Services Administration, US Department of Health and Human Services, 2002, 11, http://store.samhsa.gov/shin/content//SMA13-4213/SMA13-4213.pdf.

CHAPTER 9: IS ANGER HURTING YOU?

1. According to the "Road Rage Driver Stress Profile," four potential problem areas are identified for drivers: anger, impatience, competitiveness, punitiveness.

2. Channing Bete Company, *Managing Anger: A Self-Care Handbook*.

CHAPTER 10: NO MORE EXCUSES: MYTH BUSTING

1. Patrick M. Reilly and Michael S. Shopshire, *Anger Management for Substance Abuse and Mental Health Clients: A Cognitive Behavioral Therapy Manual*, Substance Abuse and Mental Health Services Administration, US Department of Health and Human Services, 2002, 11, http://store.samhsa.gov/shin/content//SMA13-4213/SMA13-4213.pdf.

CHAPTER 11: CONQUERING INTENSE EMOTIONS

1. This is a variation of what was created by Albert Ellis in the 1950s for rational emotive behavior therapy and utilized by SAMHSA (2002) in *Anger Management for Substance Abuse and Mental Health: A Cognitive Behavioral Therapy Manual*.

2. Modified from Channing Bete Company, *Managing Anger: A Self-Care Handbook*.

CHAPTER 13: BEGIN AGAIN

1. Corrie ten Boom, *Clippings from My Notebook* (Nashville, TN: Thomas Nelson, 1982).

CHAPTER 14: BREAKING THE CHAINS THAT KEEP US BROKEN

1. These verses cause confusion for many, and I make no claim to be an expert, but it's clear this is not referring to remission of sin. Romans 10:9 states, "If you declare with your mouth, 'Jesus is Lord,' and believe in your heart that God raised him from the dead, you will be saved."

2. L. Gregory Jones, "Forgiveness" in *Practicing Our Faith*, ed. Dorothy Bass, quoted at "Learning to Dance," Inward Outward, April 7, 2016, http://inwardoutward.org/quote-source/forgiveness-in-practicing-our-faith-edited-by-dorothy-bass/.

3. Richard Foster, *Celebration of Discipline* (New York: HarperCollins, 1988), 143.

CHAPTER 15: REBUILDING RELATIONSHIPS

1. L. Gregory Jones, "Forgiveness" in *Practicing Our Faith*, ed. Dorothy Bass, quoted at "Learning to Dance," Inward Outward, April 7, 2016, http://inwardoutward.org/quote-source/forgiveness-in-practicing-our-faith-edited-by-dorothy-bass/.

2. Lewis B. Smedes, *Forgive and Forget: Forgiving the Hurts We Don't Deserve* (San Francisco: Harper & Row, 1984), 36.

3. James Sells and Mark Yarhouse, *Counseling Couples in Conflict: A Relational Restoration Model* (Downers Grove, IL: InterVarsity), 48.

4. Sells and Yarhouse, *Counseling Couples*, 59.

5. Martin Luther King Jr., *Strength to Love* (Minneapolis, MN: Fortress, 1977), 54.

CHAPTER 16: SOLVING PROBLEMS IN A MINDFUL WAY

1. See www.mindful.org.

2. Conflict-resolution model retrieved from http://store.samhsa.gov/shin /content//SMA13-4213/SMA13-4213.pdf. The five steps for effective problem solving and cost-benefit analysis are used across the mental health field. The application here is the author's own.

3. *Cost-benefit analysis* (CBA) is a popular term used across professional fields. The application here is the author's own.

4. Merriam-Webster, s.v. "cost," www.merriam-webster.com/dictionary/cost.

5. Henri J. M. Nouwen, *The Dance of Life: Weaving Sorrows and Blessings into One Joyful Step*, ed. Michael Ford (Notre Dame, IN: Ave Maria Press, 2009), 30–31.

6. "How Meditation Helps with Difficult Emotions," *Mindful*, April 7, 2014, www.mindful.org/how-meditation-helps-with-difficult-emotions/.

CHAPTER 17: THROW OUT A LIFELINE: HELPING TRAUMA SURVIVORS

1. Carlo Carretto, *Why, O Lord?*, as cited in Rueben P. Job and Norman Shawchuck, *A Guide to Prayer for All God's People* (Nashville, TN: Upper Room Books, 1990), 179.

CHAPTER 18: REIMAGINE: A MINI RETREAT

1. Patrick M. Reilly and Michael S. Shopshire, *Anger Management for Substance Abuse and Mental Health Clients: A Cognitive Behavioral Therapy Manual*, Substance Abuse and Mental Health Services Administration, US Department of Health and Human Services, 2002, 11, http://store.samhsa.gov/shin/content//SMA13-4213/SMA13-4213.pdf.

2. James 4:14.

APPENDIX B: BONUS: ANGER CUES AND ANGER SCALE

1. Patrick M. Reilly and Michael S. Shopshire, *Anger Management for Substance Abuse and Mental Health Clients: A Cognitive Behavioral Therapy Manual,* Substance Abuse and Mental Health Services Administration, US Department of Health and Human Services, 2002, 11, http://store.samhsa.gov/shin/content//SMA13-4213/SMA13-4213.pdf.

2. Formerly available at www.alecgore.com/road_rage/quiz.html.

BIBLIOGRAPHY

Barris, B. (1999). *When Chicken Soup Just Isn't Enough: Managing Anger in an Increasingly Angry World.* SmilingWarthog Publishers.

Channing Bete Co. (2006). *Managing Anger: A Self-Care Handbook.* South Deerfield, MA: Channing Bete.

Harris Interactive (2012). Retrieved from www.harrisinteractive.com.

Ipser, J. C. & Stein, D. J. (2012). Evidence-based pharmacotherapy of post-traumatic stress disorder (PTSD). *International Journal of Neuropsychopharmacology, 15,* 825–40. doi: 10.1017/S1461145711001209.

Jarero, I. & Artigas, L. (2012). The EMDR Integrative Group Treatment Protocol: EMDR group treatment for early intervention following critical incidents. *European Review of Applied Psychology, 62* (4), 219–22.

Merriam-Webster Dictionary (2013). Retrieved from www.merriam-webster .com/dictionary/.

Moller, A. T., T. Backstrom, H. P. Sondergaard, and L. Helstrom (2014). Identifying risk factors for PTSD in women seeking medical help after rape. *Plos One, 9* (1), 1–9. Retrieved from www.plosone.org.

Potter-Efron, R. (2005). *Handbook of Anger Management.* Binghamton, NY: Taylor & Francis Inc.

Raabe, F. J., and D. Spengler (2013). Epigenetic risk factors in PTSD and
    depression. *Frontiers in Psychiatry 4* (80), 1–18. Retrieved from
    www.frontiersin.org.

Road Rage Driver Stress Profile. Retrieved from www.alecgore.com
    /road_rage/anger_beliefs.html.

The Car Connection (2012). "Study Reveals Women More Prone to Road Rage
    than Men." Retrieved from http://newyork.cbslocal.com/2012/07/27
    /study-reveals-women-more-prone-to-road-rage-than-men/.

US Department of Health and Human Services (2002). *Anger Management for
    Substance Abuse and Mental Health Clients.*